```
I0150556
```

For my brother-in-law,

CPL Nathan Brock Carse,

who taught me to be more afraid of the *status quo*
than of the future.

10% of all author royalties are donated

to the CPL Nathan Brock Carse Memorial Scholarship Fund

Copyright © 2011 by Matt Brown
All rights reserved.

Photography:
Jennie Good Photographs – www.jenniegoodphotographs.com

Layout and Cover Design:
Mélissa Caron – www.Go-Enki.com

Editor:
Richard Burian – www.Richard-Burian.com

ISBN 978-0-615-468969

The Insurance XPERIENCE

The *Ultimate* Guide
to Success for
**Young Insurance
Professionals**

MATT BROWN

CONTENTS

Praise for Matt Brown and *The Insurance Xperience*

You cannot learn from those who do not know. Matt Brown knows. In The Insurance Xperience, *Matt combines extensive research with street level sales lessons learned to write a sales primer for insurance professionals. New agents benefit from successful, time tested sales and marketing ideas. Veteran agents learn 21st century strategies that can measurably increase sales.*

Matt's ideas help jettison selling activities demanding high effort and yielding low results. He provides valuable advice on ways to attract buyers in abundance. Then, Matt offers specific examples, precise steps to follow, and narratives to master the art of delivering value when selling insurance. Be prepared to change your thinking and become an 'insurance artist' after reading The Insurance Xperience."

Ed Lamont CIC, CRM
Author of *STREET SMART SELLING: The Beliefs, Strategies, and Management Ideas of Successful Insurance Professionals*

After 42 years in the insurance industry, I have listened to countless motivational speakers, attended sales seminars, and read volumes of management related books. I found Matt Brown's The Insurance Xperience *to be a breath of fresh air.*

Matt provides the reader with a fresh perspective based on his personal experience. As an insurance industry veteran, I found the The Insurance

Xperience *a revitalizing read. Yes, Matt has laid out a practical road map for success.*

The book is filled with tips, step-by-step guides, and how-to advice. More importantly, I think this book's unique value and that which will resonate with the young insurance professional will be the real life stories and shared experiences, as well as, Matt's sincere and down to earth approach."

Rick Morgan
Consultant
www.RickMorganConsulting.com

Matt Brown has given the insurance industry a gift with The Insurance Xperience. *After reading it I have already generated more sales because of the concepts I took straight out of the book. Thank you!!"*

Ryan M. Hanley
Insurance Agent - The Murray Group Insurance Services, Inc.
Author - *Albany Insurance Professional Blog*
www.RyanHanley.com

Matt's book, The Insurance Xperience, *is an outstanding sales and career development resource providing you the tools necessary to achieve success as a leader in one of our nation's most stable and lucrative professions."*

John J. Bishop, CPCU, CLU
Chairman, President and CEO at The Motorists Insurance Group

There are two reasons why today's insurance professionals need to change their sales approach in order to stay relevant in the future: an industry that is increasingly viewed as a commodity (one-size-fits-all approach) and consumers who no longer want to be 'sold to.' Agents who not only get the job done, but add value and provide a memorable experience in the eyes of the customer, will end up creating a raving fan base that will support them, refer others and create a positive energy and long-lasting relationship. This book provides the tools to accomplish these goals. What Matt has done here is nothing short of amazing, and anyone who is serious about their insurance career would be wise to read this book and begin the path to being an industry leader."

Carrie Reynolds
"The Insurance Goddess" at Alan Galvez Insurance
www.InsuranceGoddess.com

In reading Matt's book, I truly felt as though he infiltrated my brain over the last dozen years on various issues I contended with as a younger person on the retail side of insurance. I wish I had this book about 20 years ago when I first started my career as a paid insurance professional. He speaks to you like he's sitting right next to you. You feel inspired and motivated to overcome the traditional, standard challenges and proverbial 'head trash.'"

Linda Rey
Partner at Rey Insurance Agency
Sleepy Hollow, NY
www.ReyInsurance.com
Find us on Twitter @ReyInsurance

Foreword

**James J. Kennedy, CPCU
President and
Chief Executive Officer
Ohio Mutual Insurance
Group**

The property-casualty business is a highly honorable one in which to work, as each day, you get the opportunity to interact with a wide variety of people who face a wide variety of risks as they go about their daily lives. How wonderful it is to know that when you solve one of their risk challenges, that you have enabled those people to go about their daily lives, carry on their daily activities, and in general, allow them to fulfill their dreams.

Insurance sales people enable this dream fulfillment every moment of every day. When someone needs a mortgage in order to buy their dream house, they turn to their insurance advisor for homeowner insurance. When people buy that new car they have always wanted, they talk to their insurance advisor for auto insurance protection. When a business seeks to open to sell that new product the owner has invested in, they turn to their insurance advisor for insurance coverage. When a farmer looks to plant that first field of grain, they talk to their insurance advisor for protection.

How wonderful it is to be in the position every day to enable your customers to drive to work, own a home, open the doors of their business, and grow the crops that feed us all! How powerful and personally gratifying to have this be your life work.

So, being an insurance sales person is so much more that just taking orders and waiting for people to come to you to purchase your product. As such, like a profession, it requires discipline and focus to be successful to earn the right to solve people's problems and to help them achieve their dreams.

In this book, Matt Brown provides a blueprint on how he has been successful in helping his client find their dream. He offers specific and detailed direction into the requirements of success: goal setting, attitude focus, time management, marketing, personal branding, and developing client relationships. He has jam packed this book with practical tools that can be used today to help anyone improve their insurance experience.

On page 165, Matt says: "I believe that if you want to belong to the top 10% of young insurance professionals in this industry then you are going to have to separate your selling style and philosophy from the other 90% of your competitors." Couple that with his constant references to the need for insurance agents to "create a value difference," and you have the essence of the spirit of the journey you are about to take in this book.

It has been an honor and privilege to have been able to think alongside Matt as he has prepared the thoughts that he is sharing here. He is already in the top 10% — and you can be as well! Enjoy!

James J. Kennedy, CPCU
President and Chief Executive Officer
Ohio Mutual Insurance Group

First and **Foremost**

"The young insurance professional who knows
how *will always have a* ***job**...*
But the young insurance professional who knows
why *will always be a* ***market leader**."*

– Matt Brown

MY STORY AND WHY YOU NEED THIS BOOK

"A positive attitude is a self-imposed blessing, and your job is to figure that out and bless yourself forever. Forever."

I'll never forget those words. I was driving down to my first weekend of Property & Casualty classes at PIA Ohio in Gahanna when Jeffrey Gitomer dropped that line in his audio seminar *How to Not Suck at Sales.* That forever changed me. I realized at that moment I first had to learn how to bless myself and develop a truly positive attitude. I came across Gitomer by chance – just Googled "sales training" and his site www.gitomer.com popped up on the first page.

I connected immediately with his style and approach to selling. It made sense to me. For someone like myself, who had no direct sales experience, Gitomer gave me hope. So, I took his advice and began downloading and buying every book I could on the subject of 'positive attitude'. *Why?* Gitomer said that a positive attitude is directly related to sales success; it's at the core of all success.

So I started at my core. I completely reinvented myself on the inside. It saved my marriage. It saved my life. So, I guess I have Gitomer to thank for that spark and all of the subsequent positivity and success that has resulted since.

However, I soon found out that obtaining a positive attitude took time and practice. It doesn't come overnight. And I had to start selling insurance in the meantime; there's no pause button for attitude training. I learned on the run, and I found out very quickly that the insurance industry was wide open.

In my markets and communities, every agent was pretty much the same. We sell on price. We complain about our companies' underwriting guidelines being *too* strict. We blame the economy and the market for rate increases and getting shopped by our insureds.

When all you do is focus on the negative and sell on price it's no wonder after twenty years agents look exhausted and pissed. I remember cold-calling in person for the first week on commercial accounts. One prospect commended me on going door to door as I was, but he finished by saying, "You gotta get out there and shake the bushes." What? I felt kind of cheap after he said that. I'm not sure *why* exactly; I just know I didn't want to feel like that again. So I began reading even more at night and waking up early (which was easy, because our sons were up all the time at night – three boys under the age of 5) to do more self-educating. Gitomer, Ziglar, Sandler, Lamont, Wodicka, Peale, Tracy, Godin, Chopra, Dyer, Hill, Carnegie and countless other thought-leaders became my closest friends and mentors. It became all-consuming.

I scrapped my list of 100 friends and family members to prospect and told myself I would never cold-call them. I would never even ask them about their insurance. I hated when close friends would call you up after years of not seeing each other and try to pitch you on some investment or other sales product. I didn't hate my friend, just how they approached me – as a potential sale.

I decided to write my own map and begin leveraging some of the best principles and philosophies I was learning about – things like belief and faith; the law of attraction; the principle of least effort; making friends with as many people as possible; creating and gifting my talents to my market; social media; and many others. My entire person changed. I began to do more generous acts for others – and not because I wanted something in return, but simply *to do*.

My ultimate goal was to join the top 10% of money earners in the insurance industry, and yet, still achieve the lifestyle and time to accomplish other goals in my life. Once I mastered the Principle of Least Effort and other productivity techniques, I found that I could do so much more with the time leftover in my week. Success, in the words of Earl Nightingale, is nothing more than the progressive realization of a worthy ideal. I dig that.

After only two years in the industry, I had been nominated for The PIA National's Young Insurance Professional of the Year Award. I was also contacted by PIA Ohio who wanted to interview me about what I was doing as a Next-Gen leader in the industry. I was honored. However, I was in the middle of writing my manuscript for what would become this book when my family was dealt a severe blow.

On February 8th, 2011, my brother-in-law Nathan Carse, was killed in action in Afghanistan by an IED. Nathan's decision to enlist in the Army and join as a Combat Engineer at the age of 31 was not an easy decision. It challenged the status quo and upset many of those closest to him.

Many of us — call us the *naysayers* — thought that someone with his gifts, talents, education and experience should be staying with the nice safe consultant career he had built for himself. He had recently earned a Master's Degree in Civil Engineering from Louisiana State University. He was making *bank* and paying off his student loans (which is very important). But Nathan wasn't happy with the way things were.

Nathan felt called to take his talents and share them in one of the most dangerous environments on the planet. The decision to *do* was his moment.

The action of enlisting solidified that decision to *do*. And there were several subsequent moments and decisions to *do* along the way. For example, Nathan was qualified to step in after Basic Training to assume a leadership position – a safer position. But he pleaded with his superiors to permit him to take a lower position with those he would one day lead, because according to him, "Who would want to follow someone who hasn't actually done what *he* is asking them to do?"

All of Nathan's fellow officers spoke highly of him. One noted that Nathan would always take the heavier load when others would walk away or reach for the lighter pack. One pack weighing over 70 pounds would need to be carried for hours upon end in the scorching heat and treacherous conditions – Nathan always volunteered first with a smile.

Our community rose up after the news broke and I have never witnessed such an outcry of support following the death of an individual. When we brought him home from the airport, the county roads we traveled were lined with community members and American flags.

In that moment, nearly eighteen months prior to his death, Nathan chose to *do*. A true model of challenging the status quo and doing what one is called to do is embodied in his decision. It's not easy to do something that others do not agree with. It's not easy to risk it all. It's not easy to give up what is comfortable. But that's what truly living is all about, and Nathan *truly* lived.

That's why this book is in your hands. Nathan's decision to *do* sparked something in me, long before that decision took his life. And now, in his death, Nathan's decision to *do* is continuing to encourage others to seize their moment. Every time I speak before a crowd I share his story and decision to *do*. His legacy lives on and inspires others.

There are many different interpretations of what success truly means. I believe in the words of Earl Nightingale, "Success is the progressive realization of a worthy ideal." Success doesn't mean you have to write $1,000,000 in premium this year (although, you would be pretty popular in your agency if you did). From my perspective, success means you are taking daily actions towards improving from where you are at this moment **to where you want to be**.

When I first joined the insurance industry, my objective was to find out what the best Producers were doing and achieving so I could belong to that group. I soon discovered that the top 10% of Producers were generating six-figures every year in commission. That's a financial goal, and one that I'm working towards every day. But I believe that success is <u>more</u> than simply earning a commission or crushing a quota. Success is about changing your insureds and community for the better. It's about becoming a more effective Producer. It's about helping those around you WIN. It's about doing something remarkable. And when it comes to sales, it's about constantly self-educating and learning how to effectively engage your prospect and identifying what true <u>value</u> means to them.

The top 10% of young insurance professionals are committed to self-educating daily. They read books, listen to, and attend seminars that help them continue to increase their level of success. Success is a process and a journey – not necessarily an income figure. It's also been my experience that the top 10% are committed to applying the same basic principles – which are fundamental truths. Principles, when followed like a recipe, always work. No matter what market you live in and have the privilege to serve – if you apply the principles revealed in this book, you will rise to the top 10% of your market. You will change your insureds for the better. You will do something remarkable.

This book is part of my journey towards success. Within the pages of this book are the principles, strategies, ideas, techniques and common practices of the top 10% of young insurance professionals. As you read this book, take notes and reflect often. If I could share just one truth with you about *success*, I learned from my brother-in-law CPL Nathan Carse - it is simply *to do*. Take action. Start now. This is me *doing*, my prayer is that you *do* as well.

I wish you the best in your journey towards success (and I really mean that),

PILLAR I

"BE"
IS FOR BEING THE RIGHT KIND OF PERSON

1 | **Prehistoric Thinking**

---

*"The reasonable man adapts himself to the world;
the unreasonable one persists in trying to adapt
the world to himself. Therefore all progress
depends on the unreasonable man."*

– George Bernard Shaw,
Maxims for Revolutionists

Did you know there was (and still is) an insurance policy for a pirates' ransom? Today it is referred to as a "K&R" (kidnapping and ransom) policy. If you Google "kidnapping and ransom insurance" you would be surprised at how much detail there is on the subject. It's intended primarily for people who do a lot of international travel and are perceived to be extremely wealthy.

I'm sure this coverage is required by many large shipping operations that travel the seas; but what about during the 17th and 18th centuries? I couldn't find in my research that it was *required*; although, it seemed as though the owner of a ship who carried this type of policy for his hands (employees) could leverage this as a selling point for hiring the best.

The reality was, people would go out to sea and get *into it* with a ship full of pirates trying to commandeer their contents and/or individuals for a ransom. But what happened when the insured didn't carry enough coverage? Do you think they settled *out of sea*? I don't know. I'm just asking.

I think at the beginning of anything there are a lot of kinks to iron out and mistakes to be made so you can improve. I feel bad for the individuals who had to be part of the "Kidnapping & Ransom" policy rewrites.

"Sorry Captain, our policy has an exclusion for any hand kidnapped after jumping onto the pirates' ship as an act of *swashbuckling*. It appears we don't have coverage for Leonard." And hence, the beginning of insurance fraud (I'm sure of it).

Our industry has definitely evolved for the better over the years (just ask those captured by pirates). When it comes to risk management we have always looked to spread risk over a larger number of people.

As cavemen, we learned to hunt as a group and spread the risk of being gored to death. But part of this need to survive required us to fit in, and not stand out. We learned to run away from whatever threatened us; or retaliate and fight.

THE LIMBIC SYSTEM: WHY WE WANT TO FIT IN

The problem is that we still have these inclinations seeded within our brain. This is evident by the sheer number of us who walk, talk, present proposals and give quotes in the same manner. We use the same cliché phrases on follow up calls. We use the same ACORD forms on appointments for gathering data. We prefer to sell on price by "quoting and hoping".

It's just easier to do what everyone else in our market is doing, and hell, why not blame the company for our inability to sell the policy. "Your prices are too high!" "You are too strict on your underwriting!" "The market's just crazy right now." "It's the holidays, nobody wants to talk about insurance."

Your enemy, as a young insurance professional, is YOU. Rather, a part of your brain. Your success (or failure) comes down to a system working in your brain. It is called the Limbic system. Seth Godin, bestselling author of *Linchpin*, refers to this system as your 'Lizard Brain'.

"The lizard brain is hungry, scared, angry and horny. The lizard brain only wants to eat and be safe. The lizard brain will fight (to the death) if it has to, but would rather run away. It likes a vendetta and has no trouble getting angry. The lizard brain cares what everyone else thinks, because status in the tribe is essential to its survival." (excerpt from *Linchpin*)

This voice in your head, who constantly belittles your efforts and tells you "*you can't do that*"; and urges you to take revenge and hold grudges and follow a script; this is the part of your brain we are going to train to be quiet. I am giving you permission to tell it to shut up. Part of being the right kind of person is having the right mindset. Not easily silenced, this part of your mind has two objectives:

1. To get you to remain part of the crowd, fit in, and not stand out

2. To get you to not deliver on what you truly wanted, thus making you feel like a failure and keep you inside sitting at your desk going through the motions

Here are specific examples that your Limbic system has not yet evolved (don't feel bad, this is inherent and you are going to learn how to reprogram your brain later in this chapter):

→ You're afraid to "cold call" on a business owner because he or she might be busy and you don't want to interrupt them... so you tell yourself.

→ You send an email instead of calling the prospect directly.

→ Checking your email because you think you may have missed something important or urgent (FACT: There are rarely ever real emergencies, at least not sent via email).

→ Making excuses as to why your sales have been down. ("Nobody is buying insurance during the holidays"; "This soft market is killing me.")

→ Get involved on a committee in a local organization and don't volunteer to lead or chair a project.

→ Start committees without an action plan in place.

→ Haven't taken a course to learn a new skill in years – you're the smartest person in the world, right?

→ Haven't read a book since middle school.

→ Don't voice your opinion in meetings for fear that you will be rejected and *castrated* (not a misprint) by the group.

→ Start out on fire on a particular project, and then disappear into the background without completing it.

→ Criticize other agents for doing something different and succeeding; it probably means your boss will want you to try that approach now too.

→ Being really, really busy, and yet unable to accomplish anything of significant value.

→ Push uncomfortable calls and conversations to tomorrow.

→ Always looking for the next big shiny thing, tossing what you learned yesterday to the wayside.

→ Telling yourself that great talkers are great salespeople.

→ Checking your cell phone every fifteen minutes... just because.

→ Telling yourself that great talkers are great salespersons; and you don't feel you're a great talker (HINT: The best salespeople talk about 30% of the time, or less).

→ Get anxious about what you are wearing and what others might think... "My town isn't fancy, I should dress down like the common folk around here, and I don't want to come off stuck up."

→ "The prospect told me he had been with ABC Agency for 20 years, I could've pressed him to see how loyal he really was, but I don't want to be pushy."

→ "I can't write an insurance blog, what about the E&O exposure, it's too risky."

→ "I can't do anything about it; my Principal picks my business cards and tells me how to set my voicemail."

This voice in your head is really just a whiny, pathetic pansy. The purpose of this part of your brain is to keep you safe and secure, and that's not entirely a *bad* thing. The problem is that we allow it to permeate and negatively affect our daily choices – this ultimately leads to a more discouraged, cog-like, unproductive *yet really busy* mentality. It's exhausting!

This is why people in your office complain about feeling exhausted at the end of each day, and yet, are never able to catch up with their work. The Lizard Brain has won. Imagine a large iguana wearing sunglasses standing on top of your desk beating its chest... that's how I imagine the Lizard Brain behaves when it knows it's winning.

TIP

Here is what you do when you feel the urge to do something counterproductive (like checking your email while working on a proposal):

Sit in silence and take no action. This part of your brain is going to go *ape*. However, after a few minutes, it will die down and you will be able to go back to what you were working on.

At first this will take a lot of effort on your part, and it could happen several times in one morning. Eventually, however, the Lizard Brain will begin to understand he is losing and will stop bothering you so often.

INTERNAL NEGATIVE DIALOGUE

Could you earn a living by quoting and selling on price alone? Sure you could. But do you want to be treated like an *insurance salesperson*?

We get treated like commodity all the time. People call you up? They call you up for a quote. You assume that's the way this industry operates, so you quote it up for them. But, you can't beat their current premium; or, at least not by enough that they feel inclined to switch to you, so you get the old, "We'll think about it and get back to you."

Maybe you land one out of every thirty you quote and justify it in your mind as the process you must *endure* to write business. So you just quote and quote and quote! The whole time you are doing this, compounded over twenty years, you begin to feel and reflect like someone who has been used. I know this, because I see people in the industry who simply look tired.

The conversation that they carry on in their head all day long has been consistently negative over their life. That voice has been telling them to keep on doing the same thing because to do otherwise would require them to make a fool of themselves. Stop listening to that voice in your head.

That voice is the sole reason for your current position in life. That voice keeps you subscribing to the notion that if you quote enough, success will follow. Sure, in about twenty years. And, at the expense of your reputation as an agent who QUOTES.

Don't allow that voice to keep you where you are. You have to learn to silence it. You should take the rest of today and simply listen to that voice and what it tells you to do. Any urge you get, monitor it and make a note of it.

You would be shocked at how negative your thinking is and how often you are encouraged to do things that have little to no significance in the outcome of your success as a young insurance professional.

Play-by-Play Example of Your *Negative* Internalized Voice

→ 7:30 a.m., "I really wanted to get this day off to a great start for my son but he flipped out when I woke him up and I yelled at him."

→ 7:45 a.m., "Why can't this school shovel a damn sidewalk, I'm wearing my best leather shoes."

→ 7:46 a.m., "Fantastic, now they're throwing salt on the sidewalk, that's going to ruin these shoes."

→ 8:00 a.m., "My boss just asked me where I was in my sales this month, get a life *jerk off*, it's only the 4th of the month."

→ 8:20 a.m., [checking email] "I guess I better respond to all these emails..."

→ 8:21 a.m., "I'll check my Facebook real quick..."

→ 8:46 a.m., "I better get those emails out now..."

Does that sound familiar? I have three sons under the age of five, so my mornings are chaos. Getting my oldest around for school is comparable at times to having a root canal performed. Kids amplify everything. Frustration is at every turn. Or is it? I have discovered that most of this is an internalized thing. Stress is an internal thing. Pressure is external. Pressure does not cause us to lose control or give in. We *choose* our reaction and decision in each situation that arises.

If you monitor yourself closely enough, you will also find that you talk <u>all day long</u> to yourself. It's kind of ridiculous. You justify irrational behavior and decisions that lead you away from what you truly want, *and* you feel like crap in the process. That doesn't make sense; but it's nothing new either – St. Paul understands this frustration:

> *"I do not understand what I do.*
> *For what I want to do I do not do, but what I hate I do."*
> — St. Paul, Romans 7:15

It is this kind of thinking that prevents us from joining the top 10%. Matters outside of work follow us to the office. The boss comes down on you and you start trash talking yourself again. You haven't had a sale in two months and start feeling like *not* going out of the office or engaging anyone about insurance.

Here are <u>three action strategies</u> that will help you <u>silence</u> that voice in your head, and help your Limbic System to evolve:

#1   Replace a Negative Thought With a Positive

Monitor your self-talk for one day. Whenever you catch yourself thinking something negative, instantly replace it with a positive statement. It looks and sounds like this:

Negative: "These prospects don't want me calling them up, they hate sales people and I don't blame them at all. Cold calling sucks."

Immediately, I will reverse this statement and state (in my mind):

"Stop. These prospects are going to be thrilled to hear from an insurance leader like myself who focuses on helping business owners solve insurance problems. I'm the most genuine insurance adviser I know, they will love to hear from me."

You may initially think this sounds corny. Corny is good. The trash you've been feeding your mind through your negative self-talk hasn't done you any good up to this point anyways! Believe me, the reversal strategy works. Each time you begin to say something negative to your *self*, replace it with its positive.

#2 Silence the "Little" You

When I first began speaking to audiences, I would get really nervous. *So* nervous, in fact, that I would actually carry on a conversation in my head before arriving to the venue that would go like this (actual example):

"To be honest, they probably wouldn't have a problem if you just emailed the event coordinator and told her that you got sick. Well, it would have to be specific, sick is too generic and cliché. Maybe if I called her office when I knew she would already be on her way to the event, I could leave a voice message telling her I had explosive diarrhea... I mean, who's going to argue that one?"

Even though I knew in my heart I couldn't and wouldn't bail – I was really good at making myself feel like I had a way out. Here's another example of me, giving myself a hard time before going in front of a crowd:

"These people are not going to laugh at your opening bit. You're not a comedian, dude. Just go straight into your presentation like everyone else does. In fact, you know you're going to forget some of the main parts, right? You should've practiced more."

This is nonsense. I'm really good at shooting myself down before doing something I know I can do and should do. You probably do the same. Here is how I started to respond when *that guy* raised his voice inside my mind:

Stated out loud:

"I need the *little* me to shut his mouth. The *big* me knows I am ready and prepared. The *big* me knows I practiced my butt off. And the *big* me knows I am quite, *quite* funny. I am going to nail this presentation baby!"

The one time I finally exploded on myself for getting so nervous and detail-focused on screwing up, I felt the pressure release – as if I completely shut the voice off and sent it running for the hills.

What about your appointment with the big prospect? Does your "little you" try to convince you that you are not going to walk away with a sale? Unless you correct that negativity with its positive counterpart, you will fail. It is imperative that you take your internal dialogue seriously and only partake in positive encouragement.

#3   Act As If

> *"You're so money and you don't even know it."*
> — Vince Vaughn, playing Trent Walker in *Swingers* (1996)

If you are having a horrible month, sales are down, and you don't feel like leaving the office; then you need to do the following:

Act as if you just wrote the largest account of your life. $100,000 in premium. One policy. You got the order. There is a signed check in your hand for the pay-in-full amount of $100,000. Wow! That's enormous! How would you feel? Imagine how it would feel to have written an account of that size? Let the excitement swell up in your chest and really feel it!

Now act like you are the kind of producer who writes huge premiums. Talk like that producer would talk. Walk like they would walk. Smile, because a producer writing that kind of an account would be walking away with several thousand dollars in commission even after the agency took their split. Awesome.

SAME MARKET CONDITIONS

Zig Ziglar tells this awesome story in *See You at the Top* about a very large real estate event in Michigan that he was to speak at. During the luncheon prior to his speech, he was sitting next to a man and asked him how things were going in the real estate market. The man told Ziglar that things were awful, the automotive industry was down and consequently this had a direct effect on the real estate market. He hadn't had a sale in months. If things didn't turn around soon he was going to have to find another job.

The man was so depressing that Ziglar noted even *he* began to question the message he had planned to share with the group of realtors; maybe things really were so bad that an uplifting message about self-image and goal setting wouldn't make a difference. Just then, a woman came up to Zig and introduced herself. She started to talk about how bad the automotive industry was doing at that time and Zig thought, "Oh boy, here we go again," but to his surprise she told him that she had been having some of the best sales of her career over the past few months. She even hoped that the auto industry would stay down for a little bit longer so she could keep up the great sales streak!

Isn't it amazing how within the same industry and market conditions one realtor was booming with success, and yet the other was broke and ready to quit? Did you catch the difference in their attitudes? The woman realtor was upbeat, excited and considered the down market a great thing for business; while the man realtor was depressed and beaten because of the very same market. The same applies in our industry. Doesn't matter if it's hard or soft to me. I believe that *what I do*, *how I do it*, and *what I offer* is worth the price of the policy I am offering a prospect. Do you?

2 | **Positive Attitude 5.0**

"A positive attitude is a self-imposed blessing,
and your job is to figure that out
and <u>bless yourself forever</u>. Forever."

– Jeffrey Gitomer

Being the right kind of person also means you must develop a consistent positive attitude!

Do you have a positive attitude? Many of us feel that we probably have a positive attitude some of the time. Does having a true positive attitude mean everything goes perfect and that you feel like hugging people all day long? No. I get frustrated, angry, and insecure feelings regularly. The only difference between where I was several years ago and where I am today is my reaction to those feelings.

WHAT IS A POSITIVE ATTITUDE?

A positive attitude is all about your reaction, and first impulse, to any given situation. It's also the consistent dedication you commit to the way you think.

A positive attitude is found in...

→   Your mood

→   How you talk with others (or about others)

→   How you react to rejection from prospects

→   How you respond to an angry client

→   How you answer your Principal or Sales Manager when they ask why sales are struggling

→ How you treat your kids when they spill their cereal and wake up the entire house (it's happened)

→ *How* you <u>think</u> each day!

We are born with a positive attitude, but somewhere along the way in life we lose it. I know we are born with it because my youngest son, Collin, can be sitting in a dirty diaper and <u>still</u> be laughing and smiling! That's an example, if I were sitting in my own soiled diaper I would not be smiling. The point is that our negative reactions to circumstances have been conditioned over time.

A positive attitude takes a lot of hard work to maintain. It requires that you study it and apply what you are learning. Here are several books on positive attitude that you should invest in (when you invest in a book – not spend your money – you build your own library that will become part of your legacy and character – what better gift to leave your family after you pass on than a library full of great books?).

→ *How to Win Friends and Influence Others*, Dale Carnegie

→ *Think & Grow Rich*, Napoleon Hill

→ *The Power of Positive Thinking*, Dr. Norman Vincent Peale

→ *See You at the Top*, Zig Ziglar

Start there. That's a great foundation to begin with. Many of the principles and strategies I am offering in this very book are a compilation of those four above.

A positive attitude has a direct effect on your ability to sell. When you are feeling down, sales are down. How likely are you to engage a prospect over the phone or at a networking event when you feel negative? Since we agree that it is important we learn how to begin working towards a positive attitude, let's dig in!

TAKING RESPONSIBILITY

One giant step towards creating a consistent positive attitude is to take responsibility in all areas of your life. Your first thought when a client calls up and says, "Hey we got a problem..." should be "What is the simplest and most direct solution to this problem?"

Stop Blaming Others

→ Don't blame the market conditions for lack of sales

→ Don't blame the company's underwriting guidelines (or the underwriter) for your inability to sell

→ Don't blame the agency's lack of useful resources and tools as the reason you can't sell anything

These are internal actions you can take to create a more positive environment in your mind. However, external factors play a huge role in your ability to create a consistent positive attitude.

I have outlined three specific action strategies you should implement on your journey towards creating a positive attitude:

#1 Fire Some Friends

You know who I'm talking about. Every single person has someone in their circle of influence who is dragging them down. You need to ditch them. It doesn't matter if they are your best friend since grade school – why do you think you are the way you are? You are a direct reflection of the people you associate with. I'm not advocating you call them up and tell them "You're fired!" all Trump-style. Distance yourself from them at first.

Once you begin thinking and doing things differently (because of the books you begin reading) you will begin to attract new friends. These new friends just seem to pop up out of nowhere... but the reality is, they have always been there and you are just now open to connecting with them.

I transitioned out of a lot of "friendships" when I began on my journey in early 2009. But you know what? I'm fine with that. Because now when I run into those old "friends" and we chat briefly, I discover they still have the same complaints and attitudes. Nothing has progressed. That's tragic. There are people who move from one crisis to the next each day... most are self-inflicted and created in their own mind. Fire them and thank me later.

#2   Forgiveness

I'm talking about both sides here – I recommend you approach anyone you have had a negative situation with and tell them, "I'm sorry, I was wrong, and I don't want to live with this burden anymore." These could be people from over 10 years ago. You may think they have forgotten (and maybe they have), but people need resolution and closure. Reaching out to people you have harmed (or harmed you) in the past has a tremendous effect on your overall being. You will feel a huge burden lifted off your chest and will smile genuinely for the first time in a long time.

#3   Perform Selfless Acts

Deepak Chopra says we should give a gift to each person we come in contact with everyday. That seems daunting at first glance – but it's doable. Here's what you can give:

→   A smile

→   An idea

→   A compliment

→   A silent prayer for the other person

→   A referral

→   A flower

- → A sincere handshake
- → The gift of listening intently to the other person
- → A tip regarding insurance

Each of these costs you nothing – and yes, I mean you should rip a flower out of the ground and give it to someone. Kids do this all the time and they get put in vases in prominent places in the home – you don't have to drop $50 on flowers! The goal is to give freely of yourself to others.

I'm not talking about favors either – favors incur an obligation on the recipient's end. So don't think, "Well, I'll scratch your back if you scratch mine," because that is not positive – that's selfish.

As a young insurance professional you could share some insurance advice with someone simply because it would be helpful for them, even though you know they may not hire you as their agent. That's part of your knowledge and sharing it is a gift. In *Pillar III | Create*, you will learn about *The Insurance Quadrant of Art* and how you can attract more ideal clients through gifting of yourself through specific techniques.

GARBAGE IN → GARBAGE OUT

How Television Is Killing Your Productivity and Attitude

I used to watch reruns every night after work. I'd come home, eat dinner with my wife and son and then watch *Everybody Loves Raymond* and *Seinfeld* all evening. Four hours per night watching TV. That's the equivalent of 26 full work weeks – sitting on my couch watching television. Waste.

Once I began my journey towards my positive attitude I noticed I would have ups and downs. It was really frustrating. I monitored everything I did for several weeks, and found that even though I was watching only about 90 minutes of television per day now, it was still garbage.

I found that the news and horror movies (which my wife and I watched on occasion) had subtle effects on my thinking habits. I eliminated the news and horror movies all together. After only a week, I felt significantly better! Something felt more solid within me.

Here is what I recommend, in regards to watching TV:

#1 Stop watching the news – there is honestly no reason for you to watch the news. Yes, I'm referring to your local news. Yes, I'm also referring to national news. "But Matt, how am I supposed to be informed of what's going on in the world?" You don't need to be informed. I get enough national news updates from people who barf all over me in the morning.

If people ask me about current events in politics or war, I tell them, "I have no idea..." And I'm fine with that. I care about people getting killed and tragedies taking place all over the globe; but if I'm negative as a result, what good is that to the thousands of others I had the potential of positively impacting that day?

However, keeping up on business news pertinent to our industry is a good thing! PIA and the Big "I" are two wonderful organizations that offer many great resources for current events in our industry. Take 10 minutes each day to simply <u>read</u> in the industry.

#2 If you *must* watch TV or movies, don't watch Drama or Horror. Your life has enough drama, why would you want more of it? Worse yet, horror and *slasher* movies cause nervous tension and cause tiny tears in your stomach lining. It's not healthy folks. Cut it out. Instead, I recommend you watch comedy. I now watch stand-up comedians any time I actually sit down to watch television. We're also big on any movie by Pixar in our home, these movies make you laugh and feel good inside. And the best part of these "kid" movies is that they are all uplifting and encouraging! They are success stories! This too has a subtle effect on your subconscious. You begin to believe that success is possible. Why do you think kids are so optimistic? Positive in ➔ positive out.

"Humor is sales medicine."
— Jeffrey Gitomer

HOW TO START AND END YOUR DAY FOR SUCCESS!

The Ultimate Morning Routine

What's your morning routine? Do you roll out of bed, begrudgingly and exhausted? Skipping breakfast? I'm going to share three simple (and yet highly effective) techniques you can immediately insert into your morning routine to help in developing your positive attitude:

1) Ziglar calls his alarm clock an "opportunity clock" – the fact that it is loud and annoying shouldn't bother you when you consider that you are ALIVE! Consider any day above ground a *good* day, a day for a new opportunity! In Ziglar's *See You at the Top*, he recommends you do the following upon waking to your "opportunity clock":

   A – Turn off the "opportunity clock".

   B – Immediately swing your legs around off the bed.

   C – Place your feet firmly on the floor in front of you.

   D – Jump up out of bed enthusiastically.

   E – Shout, "Yes! This is a GREAT day!"

   Now, when I first read Ziglar's recommendation I literally laughed out loud. Not only would I wake my wife (and my sons) but I can guarantee they would not be happy with me! So he offered this solution for those of us who can't yell out loud.

A – Turn off the "opportunity clock".

B – Immediately swing your legs around off the bed.

C – Place your feet firmly on the floor in front of you.

D – Jump out of bed quietly.

E – Mouth, "Yes! This is a GREAT day!" and pump your fists.

This version makes me laugh even harder – I actually did this for a couple mornings and found out that was the entire point of the exercise... to laugh at yourself and start the day in the spirit of fun. It's your call on which version to use; but the bottom line is that this works!

2) Positive Word Therapy
Positive word therapy is when you repeat positive words - or phrases - that actually cause you to feel immediately better simply by stating them out loud to yourself. You can do this in the shower; while getting ready; in the car on the way to work; just about anywhere!

Examples:
• I am enthusiastic!
• I am energetic!
• I am loved.
• Thank you Father.
• I am healthy and strong!

3) Breakfast
You should consume a healthy, protein driven breakfast within 30 minutes of waking. Protein is fuel for the brain. How much protein? Aim for 30 grams – I usually consume 5 egg whites, 1 whole egg, and 2 oz of chopped up chicken breast in the form of an omelet. My carbohydrate

source is typically oatmeal, but you could opt for any *slow carb* (Google it). Our country has turned into a frosted, sugar-coated nation for cereal – that will just slow you down. Eat a solid breakfast every morning.

REPROGRAM YOUR SUBCONSCIOUS WHILE YOU SLEEP AND ATTRACT SUCCESS

Your bedtime routine is very important to how your positive attitude progresses. Just before you drift off to sleep, your mind is in a very impressionable state – specifically, your subconscious mind. Your subconscious mind is like the operating system within you. You give it the commands through your self-talk (positive or negative) and it takes the command and acts upon it. When you begin to master this reality, you will find that true faith is belief and passion in the certainty of any one thing – and that kind of faith manifests anything you can think of into a reality (good or bad).

When drifting off to sleep, your subconscious is like a sponge ready to absorb whatever you give it. For those of you who work out, it's similar to that "window" of opportunity up to 30 minutes after training for you to consume a proper protein and simple carbohydrate shake for maximum muscle building results. Think of this as a 5-10 minute window for mental training.

First of all, before this 5-10 minute window, you must clear your mind and here is how:

→ Write out everything you must do the following day. Anything and everything that comes into your mind. If it pops up in that head of yours, write it down on your tablet.

→ Take your list of tasks to complete the following day and plug them into your *Daily Timeline* (which you will find in Step 2 | "Do").

This will clear your mind and slow it down – now you should lay flat on your back in bed and take some deep breaths to relax yourself. If something pops up in your mind again, simply write it on your tablet.

Once your mind is empty, do the following:

#1 Write your *SMART Primary Producer Goal(s)* in a notepad that you keep next to your bed. This will be discussed in the next chapter.

#2 Repeat your *Belief Statement* (once again, we will cover this in the next chapter) and closely follow all the steps regarding this Belief Statement. It is imperative you leverage visualization, faith and powerful emotions at the same time.

#3 Mental Movie Method
    Create a positive movie-like experience in your mind where you are seeing the final product of the successful you. What do you look like? How confident do you appear? What clothes are you wearing? What are you saying? What are you driving? What success are you experiencing? Be vivid and detail-specific. Incorporate all the senses. Incorporate all positive emotions tied to the experience(s) you are creating in your mind.

If you are envisioning the experience of the big prospect saying "yes" to you and your proposal, visualize the check in your hand. What does the check feel like? What does it smell like? What emotions are you feeling? This is what you will fall asleep to. <u>Good</u> night.

3 | Turning Thoughts into Things

"Give me a stock clerk with a goal and I will give you a man who will make history. Give me a man without a goal, and I will give you a stock clerk."

– James Cash Penny,
founder of J.C. Penny

.

If I could only share one chapter of this book with you – it would be this *very* one. This chapter will help you identify what you truly want; how to formulate that desire into a magnetized statement; and powerful techniques for creating the reality you desire. Being the right kind of person requires you to not only have dreams, but to implement action strategies in your life!

Goals are what we *intend* to accomplish. However, without properly defining your goal(s) – you will struggle to accomplish anything. My studies of goal achievement and ultimate success have led me to compile a *5-Step Method* for identifying, describing, writing, attracting and having any goal I have set for myself.

5-STEP METHOD FOR ACTUALIZING YOUR GOALS

Step 1 | Ask THE Question

Whether you have just joined the industry as a Producer, or you have five years of experience, we are going to start all over. You need to ask yourself one specific question:

"What do I want?"

You have the best job in the world. A Producer's responsibility is to "produce" new business. You may think you are only "sales" but today the best Producers are a hybrid consisting of sales, service, marketing, PR, and so forth. I have not yet met a Producer who told me they were capped on the amount of commission they could earn. Why would a Principal want to cap you? Your only purpose is to "produce". That's awesome!

So when I ask you, "What do you want?" your mind should begin to really dig deep. Right now, you are probably trying to hit a quota that your Principal or Sales Manager gave you. Screw the quota. You can do better.

Here is how I answered that *very* question in 2009:

"I want to be in the top 10% of insurance professionals in the world."

I have found that the top 10% of any industry is where all the money is. Don't get me wrong, I'm not a greedy person when it comes to money and tangible things, but the fact is – when you need money there are very few substitutes.

Step 2 | What Is Your Purpose

> *"There is one quality which one must possess to win, and that is*
> *definiteness of purpose, the knowledge of what one wants,*
> *and a burning desire to possess it."*
> — Napoleon Hill

Your major definite purpose in life is what God created you for. What are your gifts and talents? How can you use what you have been given to improve this world? This purpose is *beyond* insurance. It's who you are and what you do all of the time.

This requires some reflection and thought on your part. It could take several weeks for you to determine your major definite purpose. Take the time to make a list of your talents; gifts; desire to help others; etc. Get to the root of your purpose in life.

My *major definite purpose* reads as follows:
> *"My major definite purpose in life is to challenge the status quo and gift my energy,*
> *creativity and expertise to the marketplace ultimately helping others stop, think,*
> *consider and become better."*

Everything I do, therefore, is focused on my major definite purpose. And once you write your Belief Statement, you will see how this plays a vital role in attracting in detail what it is you truly want.

Step 3 | Your *Primary Goal*

Your major definite purpose in life is all-encompassing. It shines through everything you do. It is you. You are living it in each decision you make.

Your *Primary Goal* (PG) is specific to your insurance career. You can have several goals, simply apply the following steps for each goal you have. For the purpose of this book, you are going to focus on a <u>commission earnings goal</u>.

Keep the following in mind when formulating your *PG*:

→   It must align with what you really want.

→   It must align with your major definite purpose in life.

→   It must be a big goal to get the blood flowing in your mind... but not too ridiculous.

→   It must be specific.

→   If you do have other goals (which I hope you do), it should not conflict with those.

Formulating your *Primary Goal* into statement form:

A quota is not a *PG*. If you want to belong to the top 10% of producers, you will need to think and act like one. Quotas are, at best, a minimum needed to earn a *living*. The problem with quotas is they give us a mental ceiling and consequently cause us to limit our efforts.

If you have ever put a baby pumpkin in a mason jar and watched it over a period of time, you will find that it grows to fit the jar... and stops. The same thing happens with your mind and a quota – you will hit it and stop. Or worse, you will not even hit it!

A top 10% earner in this industry sets an annual **commission** goal of six figures. Your quota is most likely based on premium revenues. Hitting a quota will not take you to the top 10% of producers in this country. And besides that, you could meet your quota every month and be broke for years! Eliminate "quota" and "premium" from your vocabulary. Focus on commission as this leads to your income! How much money do you want to earn this year? A top 10% earner would say, "I earn $100,000 this year in commission."

Let's assume a 15% **commission** rate – that would mean she would need to write $666,666.67 in premium. But she isn't going to set a premium goal. She's setting an income goal – a *commission* goal! For some of you reading this, it'll require a shift in the way you think, that is, moving from thinking in terms of **quotas** and **premium**, and instead in terms of **commission** and **income**. Does this mean you must set a goal to earn $100,000 this year in commission? Of course not. But that's what the top 10% across the United States are producing each year in commission. Maybe your market isn't as large as others. Maybe $100,000 seems too daunting at first. But if you earned $25,000 in commission last year then you should at least set a goal to double it this year!

What happens when you set a commission goal, especially a larger one that gets your juices flowing? You begin to prospect differently. You spend less time chasing after accounts you know you have no chance of writing. You begin to position yourself in your market differently. Your whole style of thinking changes. So let's look at how you can capture your income goal in writing. In order to be well-received by your subconscious mind requires a SMART formula.

SMART is an acronym that defines an effective writing method of any goal that is positively received by the subconscious mind. See below:

S - Specific
M - Measurable
A - Action-Oriented
R - Reachable
T - Time Sensitive

Assuming a 12-month goal, your *SMART PG* would sound something like this:

"I earn $100,000 in commission by December 31, 2011."

Your *SMART PG* is in action-format and has a deadline. Deadlines are imperative for creating a sense of urgency in your mind. Don't ever write, "I will _____..." because that tells your subconscious it is <u>yet</u> to be done.

I wrote my goals in this "I will _____..." format for several months before discovering Brian Tracy's *GOALS!* - which drastically changed my goal writing habits and attraction rate. HINT: Invest in that book.

Write Your *SMART PG* <u>Daily</u>

Many people set a goal on January 1st and don't revisit it until the end of the year. Amazingly, they are still able to have a marginally successful year just by writing out their goal on January 1st.

Some write their goals each month. That is better. But what I found to be most effective was to write my *SMART PG* every morning upon rising, and every night before bed.

Step 4 | 50 Action Steps

"I'm tired of dreaming. I'm into doing at the moment.
It's, like, let's only have goals that we can go after."
— Bono, U2

Now that you know what you want, you have your <u>major definite purpose</u> in life, and you know your *Primary Goal*, it's time you create your map.

Make a list of 50 things you could do that would move you towards this *PG*. Just start writing. Don't think, "Well, that's really not that big of an action step so I won't write it..." Just write. Some actions or tasks that you list will actually be sub-actions of other actions – you will prioritize and structure this list soon.

Here's an example of your *SMART PG*:

I earn $100,000 in commission by December 31, 2011.

List of 50 Action-Steps

1. Determine my niche markets.
2. Compile a list of 50 suspects that are in my niches.
3. Obtain a Reference USA membership log-in for their online database for gathering some initial data.
4. Google search each suspect.
5. Facebook search each suspect decision maker and/or business.
6. Linkedin search each suspect decision maker and/or business.
7. Scrub my list based on initial data gathering and background searching and identify prospects.
8. Write my sales letter.
9. Get published in the local paper.
10. Invite prospects to a free seminar that I will perform.

And the list goes on... *What*? You thought I was going to give you 50 action steps? This is your *PG* – create your own map.

Prioritize Your Action Steps

Which step should be completed first? Go down your list and prioritize each action-step as you see fit. I would begin by defining my niche markets – this is a good starting point for any PG that is focused on new written policy premium.

This particular action step should be rewritten as follows:

I compile a list of all niche markets I intend to pursue by 12 p.m. today.

Immediate **Action Steps**

Then, follow it up with three action steps you need to take to help you accomplish the task:

I compile a list of all niche markets I intend to pursue by 12 p.m. today.

→ **1.** *I list all risks I can write competitively with my markets.*

Action Step 1

→ **2.** *I list my hobbies and personal interests.*

Action Step 2

→ **3.** *What products overlap with my hobbies and personal interests?*

Action Step 3

In *Action Step 1*, for example, you have several sub-tasks to complete in order to satisfy it. Perhaps you will make a list of questions to ask your underwriters about which products are selling; or, maybe they have them listed on their website (this would save you time). Find out *specific* underwriting guidelines for each competitive risk.

You have identified, in *Action Step 2*, the need to find out what your own personal hobbies and interests are. If one of your passions is working out, and you belong to a fitness center or gym, then I would recommend you put that on your list.

Are you going to be able to connect a little easier with a decision maker who owns a gym when you're able to speak their lingo? Of course! So in this step, you need to have fun and write down everything you like to do and determine where you would need to go to find a product that would fit this risk's needs.

Action Step 3 is about connecting your hobbies and personal interest niche markets with the ones your company (or companies) are able to write competitively. I recommend you also connect with your surplus line underwriters and find out what their appetite is – many of my niche markets were not on one of our direct carriers' list of risks they were willing to underwrite.

Once you have your three Action Steps identified, you are able to work seamlessly on a task moving from one action step to the next. In *Step II | "Do"*, you will learn more about effective use of time in your day so that you can accomplish *more* in <u>less</u> time!

For the rest of this chapter, we are going to focus on maximizing your efforts and *attracting* your goals to you quicker than you ever imagined possible. This may require a new frame of mind and thought process on your part. Believe me, this next step is the most important ingredient of your success.

Step 5 | Belief, Desire and Faith

> *"Whatever you ask for in prayer,* **believe that you have received it,** *and it will be yours."*
> — Jesus Christ, Mark 11:24

When I start talking about prayer and faith I'm betting that many of you are internally concerned that this is turning into an altar call. *Not at all.* However, I highly doubt that anyone has ever shared with you what effective prayer sounds like, and what faith *really* means. Those words get tossed around so much in religious circles that their meaning has become assumed. I feel the need to redefine how these two actions – prayer and faith – play a vital role in our success, not only as young insurance professionals, but as human beings.

First of all, faith requires several elements in order to truly be effective in assisting you to get a desired result. I personally love the story of the Centurion in Luke 7: 1-10; read the passage and note the underlined words.

> **1** When Jesus had finished saying all this to the people who were listening, he entered Capernaum. **2** There a centurion's servant, whom his master valued highly, was sick and about to die. **3** The centurion heard of Jesus and sent some elders of the Jews to him, asking him to come and heal his servant. **4** When they came to Jesus, they pleaded earnestly with him, "This man deserves to have you do this, **5** because he loves our nation and has built our synagogue." **6** So Jesus went with them.

He was not far from the house when the centurion sent friends to say to him: "Lord, don't trouble yourself, for I do not deserve to have you come under my roof. 7 That is why I did not even consider myself worthy to come to you. <u>But say the word, and my servant will be healed.</u> 8 For I myself am a man under authority, with soldiers under me. I tell this one, 'Go,' and he goes; and that one, 'Come,' and he comes. I say to my servant, 'Do this,' and he does it."

9 When Jesus heard this, he was amazed at him, and turning to the crowd following him, he said, "I tell you, I have not found such great faith even in Israel." 10 <u>Then the men who had been sent returned to the house and found the servant well</u>.

This story shares the basic principle of faith – *certainty of belief in a desired outcome.*

> *"Faith is the bird that sings when the dawn is still dark."*
> — Rabindranath Tagore

Believe that you've already received what it is that you desire. If you desire to earn $100,000 in commission, don't concern yourself with all of the details and naysayers; simply believe you've already received it. What would it feel like to have $100,000 in your bank account? The swelling up of excitement in your chest should be taking place – that's a needed emotion to attract and create the outcome you desire.

I want to share an excerpt regarding faith, from *Think & Grow Rich* – read this carefully:

All down the ages, the religionists have admonished struggling humanity to "have faith" in this, that, and the other dogma or creed, but they have failed to tell people *how* to have faith. They have not stated that "faith is a state of mind that may be induced by self-suggestion."

In language which any normal human being can understand, we will describe all that is known about the principle through which faith may be developed where it does not already exist.

Have faith in yourself; faith in the Infinite.

Before we begin, you should be reminded again that:

Faith is the "eternal elixir" which gives life, power, and action to the impulse of thought!

The foregoing sentence is worth reading a second time, and a third, and a fourth. It is worth reading aloud!

Faith is the starting point of all accumulation of riches!

Faith is the basis of all "miracles," and all mysteries which cannot be analyzed by the rules of science!

Faith is the only known antidote for failure!

Faith is the element, the "chemical" which, when mixed with prayer, gives on direct communication with Infinite Intelligence.

Faith is the element which transforms the ordinary vibration of thought, created by the finite mind of man, into the spiritual equivalent.

Faith is the only agency through which the cosmic force of Infinite Intelligence can be harnessed and used by man.

That small portion of *Think & Grow Rich* helped someone like me, who had lost the glimpse of what faith *truly* means, once again grasp and believe. The principles I learned by reading that book have proven to be invaluable in all areas of my life. Hill goes on to share that thoughts are indeed things and if we use them in our favor we can literally create the life we want to down every detail. That's a gift from God. For you to be the right kind of person you must begin to view *faith* as an action.

You can reprogram the way you think by utilizing a very simple formula offered in the pages of *Think & Grow Rich*. I altered this formula to fit the needs of me – a young insurance professional who wants to belong to the top 10% of the industry back when I first joined (only two years ago). I want to share this formula for faith building and attracting success with you.

Look at how this formula works based on your example *PG*:

HOW TO PROGRAM YOUR SUBCONSCIOUS FOR INSURANCE SALES SUCCESS

1 | Fix in your mind the exact amount of commission you want to earn. This will reflect your PG, assuming you set a commission/income goal. In the example in this chapter, it would be $100,000 in commission.

2 | Determine what you are willing to <u>give</u> in return for the premium you intend to write. There is no such thing as something for nothing. You *gotta* give in order to get. What are you willing to give in return? Whatever is fair according to the confines of your mind *is fair*.

For example, in return for $100,000 in commission you may decide that you will use your creativity for providing a unique experience for prospects and clients. You don't actually have to know *what* you will do specifically, just be open to the world and it will send the ideas to you on their own accord. (This is one of the first principles of faith – *trusting*.)

3 | Set a deadline for the date in which you intend to possess this commission income in total. This is part of your *SMART PG* statement so it should already be established.

4 | Create your **BELIEF STATEMENT**

Write out how much you desire to sell, the deadline to sell it by, and what you will give in return for it. See the example below:

By the 31ˢᵗ day of December 2011, I earn $100,000 in commission, which comes to me in various amounts from time to time throughout the interim.

In return for this commission, I give the most efficient and creative service of which I am capable, by helping restaurant owners and web developers solve their insurance problems.

I believe that this commission is in my possession. My faith is so strong that I can now see this money before my eyes. I can touch it with my hands. It is now awaiting transfer to me at this time, and in the proportion that I deliver the service I intend to render in return for it.

I trust that I am shown specific businesses that require my help and that I act immediately upon any prompting when it is received.

I recommend you do the following with your Belief Statement:

Print it on several 3x5" index cards; tape one copy to the bottom of your computer monitor, another near your bed, and a third copy should be kept on you at all times in a shirt pocket, etc. This is the <u>minimum</u> required. I put my belief statement everywhere for constant reinforcement. It should consume you.

5 | Recite Out Loud *and* Often

As mentioned a few lines prior, put one copy by your bed to read each night prior to falling asleep *and* upon waking up. Read it to yourself at lunch. Read it often. Memorize it. It should become so much a part of you that you become consumed with the agreement you are establishing with yourself.

You are reprogramming your subconscious mind, and by doing so you become a human magnet for what you desire. For those of you in doubt, refer back to the portion regarding Faith – if you doubt anything in this chapter it's proof that the *Lizard Brain* is at work in your life and that your faith is not strong. Focus on the steps we outlined earlier for helping your mind transition out of negative and doubtful thought patterns. The sales success you desire is as simple as believing you already have what you want, trusting the ideas that come to your aid throughout your journey, and taking immediate action on those ideas.

✕CHALLENGE | TICK-TOCK

Michael Michalko's *Thinkertoys* is an excellent book with exercises designed to help change the way you think and become more creative in the process. I feel that the exercise Tick-Tock is a great starter for getting your mind wrapped around the challenge in this section. It is normal to want to be normal and fit in. However, to belong to the top 10%, you must be willing to think differently. This exercise will help you write out your fears, confront them head-on and then substitute positive factors that allow you to succeed and overcome that part of your brain that doesn't want you to move.

STEP 1

Zero in on and write down those negative thoughts that are preventing you from realizing your goal. Write them under "Tick."

STEP 2

Sit quietly and examine the negatives. Learn how you are irrationally twisting things and blowing them out of proportion.

STEP 3

Substitute an objective, positive thought for each subjective, negative one. Write these under "Tock."

I have included an example sheet below that was one of my original ones when I first began this exercise and faced the challenge of overcoming my fears.

My primary fear when joining the insurance industry was <u>cold calling</u>. After a closer look, it became apparent that I was afraid of *rejection* more than anything.

TICK	TOCK
Calling these prospects on the phone and asking about their insurance is a waste of time. They have probably been with the same agent for 20 years and don't want to talk to some young, inexperienced guy like me.	If they've been with the same agent for 20 years that's great news, it means the incumbent has had 20 years to screw it up. The prospect will appreciate my authentic and sincere approach to wanting to help improve his insurance experience. I will write down all of the possible objections I could expect from the prospect and my responses to each.
The last time I cold called, one guy told me "insurance agents are all the same, don't call me again," and I really don't feel like getting treated like crap again.	I take things too personally. My approach was all wrong last time, I was only thinking about me and the sale. This time around, I only care about helping the prospect solve problems, if I can't do that for him then I'm not going to waste his time.
There is no way I'm going to get a sale by cold calling these people. They hate hearing from me; I'm just an interruption in their busy day.	I'm really insecure and unconfident. Pull it together, bro. You aren't trying to make a sale on the cold call, just feeling them out and trying to get an appointment to determine if and how you can help. Why would they hate hearing from you? You are a locally respected member of the business community volunteering your efforts constantly. Quit being a pansy and do something about it Nancy.

Obviously, you don't have to be as blunt with yourself as I am... but I *highly* recommend it. This technique really puts things into perspective; and you begin to realize that the voice in your head telling you to just fit in and not to do anything that would attract attention is not really YOU.

When you feel as though you shouldn't do something because it is going to be uncomfortable or draw unnecessary attention, this could actually be your opportunity to do something of significance that will spark a series of events that could drastically change your circumstances (and sales) as a result.

And besides, just as in this example, you can see that rejection does not exist. You had nothing before you set out to engage the prospect, so if they say "no" it's not as though you lost anything. You are in the same condition and shape as before.

PILLAR II

"DO"

IS FOR DOING
THE RIGHT THINGS

4 | The Argument for Effectiveness

"It is vain to do with more what can be done with less."

– William of Occam (1300-1350),
originator of "Occam's Razor"

Once your interior is on purpose, your exterior will begin to follow. Ever walk into someone's office and it's just a mess? Papers stacked up; files going to the ceiling on their back credenza; maybe even food wrappers on the floor next to the desk? Oh, I'm sorry, is that your office? Remember, this is a responsibility lesson – I'm writing this to YOU, for YOU. *Not* for Larry in accounting. YOU.

A mind on purpose *and* <u>organized</u> will begin to mirror itself on the outside. Your work space, whether it's an office or cubicle, needs to reflect organization. Oh, you've got a system? You know where everything is, I see. Doesn't matter to me. Doesn't matter to me if you claim to be the master of multi-tasking, which our Millennial generation claims to be the best at.

If I'm the Principal of my agency and I'm hiring a new producer, multi-tasking is **NOT** a skill I would want to see on their resume. It means you do many things at once. Some people call that being efficient. I don't care about efficiency because it doesn't sell insurance. I'm talking about being highly effective in what you do. Being effective means you are completing action steps that move you closer to your *SMART PG*. Efficiency is simply performing a task in the most economical manner possible – doesn't mean you are actually working on tasks of importance.

Checking email while you are on hold with an underwriter, while also IM'ing a buddy on Facebook doesn't make you effective. Servicing one account (like removing a vehicle from a policy online) while taking a text message on your phone and then remembering to shoot out a quick email to another client and pulling up your Outlook to do so... waste of time.

Studies have shown that distractions from the task at hand will set you off course for up to 45 minutes. And we do this all day long! What makes matters worse is that you feel really, really busy. You're so busy, in fact, that you often don't get all of the work completed that you wanted to get done that day. And when people ask you how things are going, you say, "Great! I'm really busy." You get this feeling of self-worth for working "so hard," you're exhausted by how hard you are working!

Let's say you take an hour lunch (which is ridiculous first of all, unless you are eating with a prospect or client) and you finish early. You have about 30 minutes before your conference call or meeting with the agency principal. What could you do?

Well, you could go on Facebook, check your wall feed, the notifications, see if anyone commented on your post earlier. Go over to your blog and see if there were any comments. If there were, you would reply back, *very quickly*. You might even post a thought-provoking quote as your status (after Googling "thought provoking quotes")! Now, this feels really productive to most of us.

But what did you accomplish? What if, instead, you wrote down several ideas that could help your agency reach a new niche market? Or, what if you captured (in writing) a few ideas for streamlining a process in your agency that would help reduce effort and save time for everyone? How much more effective would your meeting with your Principal be? Think that kind of value would position you as leader in your agency? I believe so.

The problem is that social media and its tools (which can be leveraged for success) encourage you to continuously check updates and comments. You poke the system and it smiles back at you, so you keep poking away. While you are poking and checking for comments and "likes" you miss out on doing the things that will take you to the top of your market in very little time.

I am going to show you how you can accomplish your *SMART PG* in half the time it currently takes you to fall short of your quota! True story.

THE ULTIMATE 1-2 PUNCH FOR APPEARING SUPERHUMAN

"As to methods there may be a million and then some, but principles are few. The man who grasps principles can successfully select his own methods. The man who tries methods, ignoring principles, is sure to have trouble."
— Ralph Waldo Emerson

The Top 10% Only Focus On 20%

This Principle changed my entire perspective of how I do what I do each day. Formerly known as The Pareto Principle because of an Italian economist named Vilfredo Pareto who noted that in 1906 nearly 80% of the land in Italy was owned by only 20% of the population. He began to look at other places in his life, like his garden, and discovered that 20% of the pea pods contained 80% of the peas! Soon, he began to note that this imbalance was in practically every aspect of life.

I began to think about the things I was doing each day at the office, and identifying where 80% of my sales were coming from. What actions were involved in those 80% of successes? Who were the 20% of clients that made up 80% of my sales? It was pretty amazing how in my first year I wrote over 70 policies but only ten of those accounted for nearly 80% of the total premium sold. I was spending a lot of time working on policies that were bringing in little to no commission, which is important when you have three children at home.

I recommend that you look closely at your own book of clients. List them out on paper. Include each policy, the premium associated with that policy, and group them. Home, Auto, Business, Commercial Auto, Umbrella, etc. Rank them from highest grossing premium to lowest. Identify the client on the policy – who are they?

What kind of business are they operating? Or what kind of associations and groups do they belong to? Are they members of local Rotary, Lions or Optimists? Do they belong to the local golf club? Find similarities and began to determine where you should probably be involved as well.

The reason is because it would make sense to continue to build upon the profitable accounts by developing relationships with like-minded individuals. Hopefully, you have some similar interests and can connect in a genuine and authentic manner.

Once I began to identify these larger account clients, I discovered that they were a lot like me! They were professionals and executives who valued their time and had similar interests. They had young families. They were entrepreneurs who had a sincere passion for doing what they loved. I clicked with these 20% of clients who were generating nearly 80% of my annual commissions and premiums.

Then I began to work logically through the types of businesses they owned or locations they lived and was able to determine my niches. Then you begin to learn how to specialize in a few lines of insurance and become more appealing to these like-minded individuals.

I would rather work smart, doing the right things, and identifying the ideal clients I can best help with my service and markets, than go out quoting randomly hoping I can write 100 accounts the next year. What if I write only 10-15 accounts that generate my *SMART PG*?

It's All In The Deadline

This is a beautiful law. It's one that many of you use and have no idea that you are using. Once you realize how it works, and you couple it with the 80/20 Principle (as Tim Ferriss suggests in his bestseller *The 4-Hour Work Week*), you will be shocked at how much you will accomplish.

I will explain Parkinson's Law with an example. If I tell you it will take you 40 hours this week to prospect and call on 50 clients, by God, you will take 40 hours to complete it. But if I tell you it will only take 10 hours, your brain kicks in and you begin to do the right things in order to complete the task at hand.

"Yeah, but the quality of your efforts are compromised, right?" No. I have studied the results of Parkinson's Law and the end result of any task with the shorter deadline is almost always of equal or even higher quality because you are extremely focused!

A personal example of this in my life as a young insurance professional would include the prospect that I engaged in several months ago about their business insurance. They didn't seem that interested but then the incumbent agent screwed up before the renewal and ticked them off, so they call me up and want to switch over to me now, possibly out of spite, who knows! But now I have to get this proposal turned around in significantly less time than I anticipated because of their impending renewal, just days away!

Aside from frustrating your underwriters (which I am not *at all* advocating) by asking to rush the proposal, I realized that it really doesn't take me that long to perform my Diagnostic Appointment, gather the necessary data from the prospect, inspect the property, fill out and submit ACORD applications, and then put everything together in my Presentation of Solutions packet. In fact, I was able (in this instance) to turn it around within a six hour time frame, thanks to the help of my underwriting team. That's *moving*.

Typically, we would draw this process out into days of effort. Separate meetings to gather data and visit properties, etc. But when focused on the task at hand and moving like you have a gun to your head, you are forced to think several moves ahead while working. Seamless efforts. Uninterrupted focus.

I have found Parkinson's Law to be the fuel needed to ultimately crushing your tasks each day! Assign shorter deadlines to all tasks. If my two PG tasks for the day include prospecting for 25 accounts online and scrubbing the list, assign a two hour limit and get it done! There are several strategies I will outline in the next chapter for how you can learn to avoid interruptions so you can focus solely on your PG Tasks before lunch, and then you can have the rest of the afternoon to work on other projects for your ultimate success as a young insurance professional.

However, I want to drive this productivity strategy home!

The ultimate 1-2 punch occurs when you leverage both the 80/20 Principle and Parkinson's Law. It is imperative that you not do just one or the other. When you do both, they become complementary of one another. People will begin to perceive you as superhuman, defying all odds and accomplishing more in a week than they are able to do in a month.

To be specific, here are your primary action steps:

Step 1: Only choose the tasks that are directly responsible for bringing in prospects who will buy, or that equate to generating revenue for yourself and your agency.

Step 2: Limit the time on these primary tasks. Severely shorten deadlines, be absolutely specific with your deadline, and work with uninterrupted focus. A proverbial "gun to the head" mindset.

Now, are you ready to learn how to train others to respect your time so you can better serve them and yourself? Let's dig in!

5 | Time: Your Most Valuable Asset

"Don't be fooled by the calendar. There are only as many days in the year as you make use of. One man gets only a week's value out of a year while another man gets a full year's value out of a week."

– Charles Richards,
Politician, scholarly lawyer, and distinguished judge

HOW MUCH IS YOUR TIME WORTH?

If you want to earn $100,000 per year, then that would mean you earn $50 per hour (based on a 40 hour work week). $50 is how much you value each hour of your workday in this instance. If you catch yourself doing something that is not leading you towards your *PG* then you are wasting money.

If you go out on an appointment and don't start by asking the prospect several key questions to determine whether they are someone you want to do business with <u>and</u> that you can help fix problems for, then you are wasting additional time... and money.

PEOPLE WASTE YOUR TIME BECAUSE YOU LET THEM

Have you ever noticed that people with nothing to do want to do it with you? It's pretty annoying isn't it? If it's not now, it will be once you start organizing and living your life on purpose. Teaching others to respect your time takes some effort and (perhaps) uncomfortable conversations at first. But it's necessary if you want to reach your PG.

Let's do this on a scenario basis and walk through how the conversation or strategy I'm suggesting would go down.

Jim is an another agent in your agency. He likes to talk, and everybody loves Jim because he tells such great stories! The only downside to this is that there are times when you have much to do but can't get focused quality work done because he would like to share a story with you!

Let's say in this particular scenario Jim stops by your cubicle (or office, lucky you) and drops one of his "Did you know..." tales.

Here is a 3-Step process for avoiding or deterring Jim so you can get your work done and not hurt his feelings.

1. By wearing headphones and focusing intently on your work, even though Jim may have just popped his head in, you can simply look up, acknowledge his presence and point down at your work with a "I'm reallllllly busy" expression. 9 times out of 10 Jim will confirm your busy expression and walk away. In the slight chance he motions for you to take off your headphones so you can hear him...

2. <u>Lead</u> with a question. As soon as I have my left headphone off my ear I will lead with, "Hey Jim, what can I help you with, I'm right in the middle of deadline." This will press Jim to consolidate his thoughts and many times will simply say, "Oh, it's nothing really, just had a great story to tell you about this past weekend." This is when he is looking for you to either perk up to hear the story or dismiss him (in the nicest way possible of course).

3. Dismiss Jim politely. If you even smile and begin to act interested he will persist and start in on his tale of excitement. As soon as Jim finishes his statement I reply, "Is there any way you could tell me after work? Right now I really do have to get this finished. Thanks." Jim, and any other person for that matter, will take the hint and understand that you are in the zone. Many times you can deter any interruption by following this simple 3-step process; step 1 is typically as far as it needs to go. Even if you aren't wearing headphones, just lead with your busy expression and ask, "How can I help you? I'm in the middle of a deadline here."

Interruptions on the Phone

If someone calls you on your cell phone during a time block when you're working and you must answer it, then do so – but get them to the heart of the message by using the following technique:

Caller: Hi, Matt? This is Bob, how's it going!

Me: Bob, things are better than good, how can I help you today?

I have learned, thanks to my oldest son Jackson, questions help people consolidate their thoughts and put them into a concise answer format, assuming you are asking the right questions.

CSR Assistance

One of the CSRs in our agency is a Godsend. When I'm working on my PG tasks for the day, I give her my time blocks I'm setting aside for completing tasks for the day. I have asked her to tell all incoming callers that I'm on a deadline but will call them back at 12:00 p.m. (if it's in the morning), or 4:00 p.m. (if it's after 12:30 p.m.).

If you have an assistant, you can do the same thing. In the following chapter, we are going to map out how we can do the right things every single day using our Daily Timeline. Remember, your time is valuable and you need to coach others to respect it as much as you do.

6 | **Daily Timeline**

"What gets measured gets managed."

– Peter Drucker,
management theorist

THE DAY BEFORE VACATION

There was a Starbucks coffee shop in one of the medical centers I worked at in my previous job. It was the place to be in the morning. Grab your coffee, chat with the other executives and managers, much like the proverbial water cooler. But on the day before a vacation or holiday, I noticed that conversations were shorter and people moved with purpose. You know why? Because they knew they wanted to get all their work done BEFORE they left for vacation or on the holiday break.

Nobody wants to come back to the office after vacation with a thousand things to catch up on. You make lists of everything that needs to be done, prioritize the list, and take ACTION! It's probably safe to assume that you get more work done on the day before vacation than you do in a typical week. What would happen if you took this approach to your office every day?"

THE $250,000 TIP

In the early 1900s, Charles Schwab (the steel titan) hired a management consultant by the name of Ivy Lee. Lee asked Schwab what it would be worth to him if his top executives increased their productivity by 20%. Schwab didn't really know how much it would be worth but that it would be definitely helpful! So Lee offered to teach them how they could do this, and in return Schwab would pay Lee whatever he felt the results were worth. After some time had passed, Schwab was thrilled with the results! He agreed that productivity had risen tremendously, and he paid Lee $25,000 – that was a small fortune in those days!

What was the secret that Lee shared with Schwab and his top executives that helped them increase productivity by over 20%? I'm going to share it with you now – first, you must write out everything you need to do the next day BEFORE you go to bed. Prioritize each task from most important to least important. And whatever task is most uncomfortable for you to perform (such as an uncomfortable conversation with a client) you must do that task first. When you wake up in the morning, and get into the office, you should begin IMMEDIATELY on your first task and move methodically from one to the next. Complete each task in its entirety. No distractions. Stay focused. You will be crushing your tasks like an animal!

Accounting for the rate of inflation over the years since Schwab paid Lee the $25,000 for this tip that would be nearly $250,000 today! You can make your check payable to "Matt Brown" and mail it to P.O. Box 205, Ada, Ohio 45810. You're welcome.

BATCHING TASKS FOR EXTREME TIME-SAVINGS

Let's say you compiled a list of tasks you must complete tomorrow. You've ordered the list from most to least important. But you have emails spread throughout the list. There's one email I really must get out first thing in the morning, it's important!

First of all, there are seldom ever any REAL emergencies. So your 'urgent' email is not really urgent. If it was, you should probably call the person.

Next, you've got several phone calls listed, some more important than others so they too are spread throughout your list of things to complete. The problem is that when you check your email sporadically, you get sidetracked. You think about how you should probably shoot so and so a quick email while you've got it open. The next thing you know, 45 minutes have gone by. Waste. You are going to 'batch' your tasks each day, and with the time you save you can do even more!

Here's how it works:

→ All emails will be checked and responded to twice daily – noon and 4 p.m. – and only 15 minutes devoted to emails each time (max)

→ All phone calls will be returned at 4:15 p.m.

→ If you must make some phone calls during the day, you should already know this in advance and we will designate a 30 minute block of time for making all outgoing phone calls

→ EXCEPTION: If you must have an <u>uncomfortable</u> conversation with an insured (or prospect) via phone, then make that call at 8 a.m. Get it over with. Then plan the rest of your outgoing calls to be made during one 30 minute block of time.

→ All applications should be filled out during one block of time

→ If possible, schedule all meetings outside the office to be on the same day so you don't have to be on the road multiple days of the week.

The key here is to set a start and end time for each group of tasks and prioritize these tasks within their groups. Set short deadlines that will make you anxious to get them done quickly. You will move methodically and free up additional blocks of time throughout your week. This extra time will come in handy later.

PG Tasks

Based on your prioritized *50 Action Steps*, required to accomplish your *SMART PG*, we will begin to outline our weeks in advance. Each week should contain ten of the *50 Action Steps*. These are the only *actions* that truly matter. You will complete two action steps per day. That's it. <u>Remember</u>, these actions steps are what we determined will move you *towards* your *SMART PG*.

Your Daily Young Insurance Professional (YIP) Timeline

At the end of each day, either the last 15 minutes before you leave the office or before bed, fill out your Daily YIP Timeline. I created this sheet over the course of two years. I have refined it on a consistent basis, but this version seems to work best.

You can create your own using Microsoft Word. The objectives remain the same – ultimate task completion and accountability. Moving seamlessly is crucial. The cool part about this daily timeline is that everything is batched by category and you choose when you will complete each batch of tasks.

I have also outlined what each category means and some examples for better comprehension.

B tasks are those that are "on deck". They are from your 50 Action Steps task list. If you get done with your PG tasks for that day, feel free to work on some other project or work ahead. This column just makes it easier to choose what will be done the next day – you just keep adding to the *B* tasks as you <u>crush</u> your *PG* tasks.

Meetings is for any appointments, chamber meetings, social/service club meetings, coffee meet ups, whatever. Basically, anything that requires you to leave the office to meet someone else OR have a phone meeting of importance. A conference call for example. A webinar. I would classify these as meetings – NOT PG tasks necessarily. In the end, listen to your gut.

Service (service work) – your agency may have CSRs who do all, or most, of your service work (except for major problems). Some agencies require that the producer service his own accounts, depending on the request.

I include a column for any service work I must complete. Drafting a proposal should be a PG Task for the day. Don't use the word "quote" or "quoting," even if you are using an online quoting system... each time you use that word it has a negative reinforcement on your subconscious. Quotes are *commodity*.

DAILY YOUNG INSURANCE PROFESSIONAL TIMELINE

- Example -

Monday, September 5, 2011
I earn $100,000 in commission by December 31, 2011.

Mission Critical	"B"	Meetings
Determine niche markets for 4th Quarter. **Start:** 9 a.m. **End:** 10 a.m.	• Scrub the list • Identify decision maker	ABC Restaurant appointment at 3 p.m.
Compile list of 50 suspects within my niche. **Start:** 10 a.m. **End:** 11 a.m.	• Use online resources to gather more data and info	Jim and Julie Smith auto/home appointment at 7 p.m.

Service	Emails	Calls
1:00 p.m. - 2:00 p.m.	12:00 p.m. - 12:15 p.m. 4:00 p.m. - 4:15 p.m.	12:15 p.m. - 12:30 p.m. 4:15 p.m. - 4:30 p.m.

Emails and *Calls*

Batch all of these tasks if possible. If you have six emails that you must send out, do that at your designated email time. Four calls to make today to current clients? Batch 'em.

BONUS: 7 FINAL TIPS FOR ULTIMATE EFFECTIVENESS!

Tip 1 | Fill in your Daily Timeline at the end of the work day or in bed before going to sleep (clear your mind.)

Tip 2 | Set start and finish times for everything you put down on your timeline. Don't be generous about it either! Remember, gun to the head.

Tip 3 | When you start your work day, begin immediately on your *PG* **Tasks**. These should be completed in the morning (if possible). Don't check email first thing, that's distracting and puts you off course.

Tip 4 | Email should be checked at 12 p.m. and 4 p.m.
Respond to all emails at 4 p.m. Remember, there are seldom any REAL emergencies. *EXCEPTION TO THE RULE*: If you are working with an underwriter on a proposal, feel free to email or call as needed.

HINT! If you don't know how to set up an auto-reply email, simply Google "how to set up an email automatic response" and this will provide you with several links to step-by-step how-to guides. In fact, be more specific in the search engine and list the client you use (i.e. Outlook, Gmail, Yahoo!, etc).

Tip 5 | Email Auto-Responder
You are going to create an auto-responder so that when someone emails you they are informed that you are working on a project, or under several deadlines, and that you will respond to their email at 4 p.m. that day.

For example:

Greetings friends,

Because I am under several deadlines, I am currently checking and responding to e-mail twice daily at 12:00 p.m. ET and 4:00 p.m. ET. If you need IMMEDIATE assistance (please be sure it is urgent) that cannot wait until either 12:00 p.m. or 4:00 p.m., please contact me directly at 419-371-7053.

I appreciate your understanding as I focus on the tasks at hand, as it will ultimately improve my clients' insurance experience.

My best,
Matt

I was in LA for an event in May 2011 and used the following for my Email Auto-Responder:

Hi! I'm in LA this week attending the James Malinchak – Big Money Speaker boot camp (www.facebook.com/JamesMalinchak) and will only be checking email once daily.

Depending on why you are trying to contact me, the following options should be considered:

→ *If you are a client wanting to make a change to a policy, forward your message to mollie@haysinsurance.net or call 419-634-5626 and ask for Mollie to assist you.*

→ *If you have an emergency, call my cell phone at 419-371-7053 and leave me a message, I will call you back at the next break.*

→ *If you would like to listen to me share some social media strategies from a recent speaking engagement, visit http://youtu.be/mUYl-GKtCQc*

→ *Download a FREE 45 page excerpt from my new book at http://theinsurancexperience.com .*

→ *Connect with me on Linkedin if you haven't done so already at http://linkedin.com/in/matthewmbrown .*

→ *Watch this HILARIOUS insurance ad http://youtu.be/HfDE45_Emog*

→ **Reply to this email** *and ask to be signed up for my weekly value ezine – an email newsletter packed full of sales, marketing, productivity and social media tips for business owners and professionals.*

Enjoy your week – I will I return on Monday, May 16th. Cheers.

Your email reply should be unique. Be yourself. Be different than everyone else. Be fun.

Tip 6 | Coach CSRs How to Answer Calls
Tell the CSRs answering phones in your agency that if someone calls for you, they are to inform them that you are unavailable at the moment but will return their call by 4 p.m.

Tip 7 | Cell Phone is Emergency Use ONLY
I mute my phone during the day. I check it around 12 p.m. and again around 4 p.m. Since I make all outgoing calls at (or around) 12:30 p.m. and 4:30 p.m. (Exception: Sales Calls) there is no reason for me to check it more often. Put the cell away. Mute it. Get the work done. The world will continue to spin on its axis.

Brian Tracy, in his book *Time Power*, notes, "Every minute in planning saves you ten minutes in execution." This is a rule of thumb, but keep in mind The Day Before Vacation scenario – if I take 15 minutes to plan out my next day, I know that I am saving nearly 2.5 hours of effort. Your Daily YIP Timeline chart should be your daily map that helps you shave off a **minimum** of 2.5 hours each day of effort.

And then, when you combine 80/20, Parkinson's Law, along with the several tips offered here, there is no reason you should ever need to work more than 10-20 hours

<u>each week</u> on your *PG* tasks. Now you have significantly more time in your day to work on projects that will help you in attracting ideal clients and mold your reputation as *leader* in your market.

This requires particular attention to how you position yourself in your market and how you intend to create the attraction. In the next Pillar you will learn dozens of strategies for positioning yourself as a market leader and influencing prospects to buy because of the *value* you bring to the table.

✕CHALLENGE | TAKE A VACATION

Sounds like a great challenge, right? But I'm serious – tell your Principal you need to take next Monday and Friday off. Use your vacation time (or not – liar). Either way, you must now complete your first ten of the 50 Action Steps you prioritized in Tuesday, Wednesday and Thursday. This is going to challenge you to eliminate everything that does not pertain to your *PG Tasks*.

Your time devoted to emails will be shortened. You will write in a more bulleted fashion. You will move seamlessly. Oh, and you can only work 8 hours maximum per day. After this three day work week, I guarantee you will accomplish more than you did in the past three months. Now you will *truly* start believing.

Are you up to the challenge?

PILLAR III

"GIFT"

IS FOR LEARNING HOW TO ATTRACT YOUR IDEAL CLIENT THROUGH ONE-SIDED GENEROSITY

7 | **Gifting & Becoming an Insurance *Artist***

"The gift is to the giver, and comes back to him..."

– Walt Whitman

What do you mean "insurance artist"? I know that's what you're thinking. Insurance doesn't really conjure up images of paint brushes and vibrant colors. That's not what I'm talking about though. Becoming an insurance artist is about doing something that changes your insured for the better. It's about creating an experience that gets talked about. It's about doing more than is expected. And it's not easy to do.

When I talk about "gifting" I mean you give freely of yourself and the experience you create for insureds. You do it because you love to do it. You don't expect anything in return because to do so would take away from the gift and the intrinsic value of the experience you create.

I believe that there are four distinct areas where we as young insurance professionals have an opportunity to create and gift our own unique forms of art. I refer to this as *The Insurance Quadrant of Art* and have outlined the opportunity in each quadrant for gifting of our art.

THE INSURANCE QUADRANT OF ART

Expertise and Advice is a young insurance professional who shares some insurance advice with a friend at a BBQ; or reviews a policy for a loved one to put their mind at ease about the coverage and price they are paying for the

EXPERTISE & ADVICE	INSURANCE SALE
SPEAKING & WRITING	WEB 2.0

policy they have, even though the loved one is not going to switch to you (tough love). You do these things because you care and because it's your area of expertise. You can offer insight that helps those closest to you and you don't charge them or put pressure on them to buy from you. That's huge. That's a gift.

Insurance Sale is when you earn a commission for selling a policy. It's the transaction that ultimately pays you a commission for selling a policy, but if you are an insurance artist, many people want to do business with you because of your value and they are willing to pay a little extra in premium knowing that working with someone like you is a WIN for them. They know that your art comes along for the ride, so they pay their premiums and you earn a commission in the process.

Speaking and Writing is an often overlooked and underutilized method for reaching a larger group of people on a personal level. Perhaps you write a monthly column in a free publication that has a 5,000 reader base. Maybe you are going to speak to the local Rotary Club about something of value that will help those in the audience produce or profit more. When you couple this strategy with the world class web 2.0 tools available (below), you are able to grow your network **exponentially**, thus enlarging the circle that is touched by your art. So not only are you generating "word of mouth", but also "*world* of mouth".

Web 2.0 is really focusing on the emergence of socialized media. You have friends, followers, and connections on all of your networks. If you invest (not spend) your time creating unique forms of art and gift them to your tribe (the collection of your friends, followers and connections) on a consistent basis, they will share your art with their friends and have an attraction towards you.

This is a gift on your part because you don't earn a dime for creating a YouTube video. But you can impact the lives of thousands of people with a click of an upload button. You don't know how far your art will reach. You don't know who it will inspire. A great example of this is best summarized in a video created by a fellow young insurance professional from Albany, NY, Ryan Hanley (www.ryanhanley.com), regarding the Wall Street Journal article that took a shot at independent insurance agents. Hanley expressed his gratitude to PIA National President Fred Thomas for standing up for independent agents everywhere and calling out the WSJ. What can you create that will connect you on an emotional level with others?

When you focus all of your efforts on the *Insurance Sales quadrant* (which the majority of insurance professionals do), your art suffers. You will become a commodity at some point. However, if you focus your efforts on the other quadrants – by gifting your expertise and talents often without expecting anything in return, you will profit the most.

There is more to gifting than just giving freely. It's not a new concept. The problem is that most of us are still carrying around an industrial and capitalistic mindset in a post-industrial era. But we are now entering a gift economy.

I recently read a book by Lewis Hyde, entitled *The Gift,* and he noted that in a commodity economy (think insurance sales – all focused on price, and policy *x* for premium *y*), status is all about how much stuff you have, how much money you have made, and how much premium you have written. In a gift economy, status is according to those who give the most to others. This doesn't mean that we give policies away for free. It means we take on a new mind, one of gifting our talents and expertise to help insureds solve problems.

In the old days, insurance agents would tell prospects that they "worked for free" as a way to get in the door and look at their policies and throw out a quote. Quoting. That's what many feel this industry is about. The more you quote the more you will write. Sure, you will write premium. But how do you feel about what you are doing? How are you truly making a difference in the insured's life?

Insurance Artists are individuals who will walk away from an account after the initial appointment because they couldn't solve any problems; but they walked away making such an impression that the prospect told five people how different you were... in a good way. People get talking. They don't understand why you won't just throw out quotes when they ask for one.

For decades the insurance industry was truly a factory, and still is in many respects. A company produces a product (policy) that they feel would meet the needs of consumers (insureds) and determine a price (fair or unfair is in the eye of the beholder) and then hire people to sell the product (you and me). If they can find someone to sell it faster and cheaper they will.

So you begin playing the numbers game and cold calling on everyone and their dog in hopes you can find some *smoking gun* (coverage error) on their old policy. You pray that the insured is with one of the companies that you know you can beat on price, and even if they aren't, hell, you'll still give them their quote. Do that for thirty years and tell me you wouldn't hate your life. I know I would. I hated it after the first six months of being in the industry.

You can see that gifting has never really been part of your nature to start with. Just because you offer to "work for free" doesn't mean you actually worked for free (if you value your time... your agency sure does). And that doesn't make it a gift either because you want to get paid for the transaction of selling insurance! So gifting is really a new mindset for most of us. It's not about scratching Jim's back and expecting him to scratch yours in return.

The true gifting cycle is best summarized by the Kula (a tribal people) who occupy the South Sea Islands near the eastern tip of New Guinea. They had a practice of gifting armbands and necklaces made from shells, which were viewed as "ceremonial gifts." They had no real value (in monetary terms) but they brought with them much coveted admiration and intrinsic value.

These gifts were passed continuously from person to person among the islands. Imagine giving your gift to the one on your right and in return you would receive from someone on your left. They were in constant motion.

You could hold on to the gift you received for as long as you like, but holding onto the gift you were given for too long brought with it much scorn and talk behind your back. The purpose was to continue the gift cycle. You enjoyed the gift for a time and then shared it with the next person, knowing that you would receive another from somewhere else.

That's the point of the gift cycle and mindset needed in this new economy we are in. Many of us hold back *giving* for fear that others will *take* our ideas and profit from them, leaving us in the dust.

Imagine gifting like that of the blood in your body, it must flow smoothly and constantly in order for us to live. Otherwise, when blocked or beginning to coagulate... you get the picture.

So what can you gift as a young insurance professional? Here are some examples of gifting from the 1st, 3rd, and 4th Quadrants:

→ Sharing insurance advice to a friend or loved one

→ Reviewing policies for a friend or loved one because they want to know if they have appropriate coverage

→ Creating a video library on YouTube for your insureds to access for common FAQs

→ A blog with helpful tips for homeowners

→ DIY (do-it-yourself) video on sump pump install and how to prevent backup into basement/crawlspace

→ Speaking to a local club or organization, sharing helpful risk management tips

→ Writing a monthly column in a small, free, local publication

→ Talking in plain English so they can understand what you mean (AKA not speaking in *insurance-iese*)

→ Sending a personalized card to a client

→ Creating and sharing a monthly ezine that helps your subscribers produce or profit more

→ The layout of your proposal and how you present it – solutions for problems, simple and clear

→ Listening to an insured complaint and calming them down while moving into solution mode

→ You streamline a process in the office (for free) that saves CSRs one hour of effort per day

→ Speaking to a local club and sharing homeowner safety tips

→ Sharing a sales strategy that works great for you with a fellow producer at another agency

→ Assisting another agent in the office (who is on a deadline) with an account you will earn no commission on

→ Calling a client to wish them a happy birthday

Like the giving nature of the Kula, give to one and rest assured that you will receive from someone else. You never really know where it will come from, but know that the universe will pay you back.

Many people thought I was wasting my time by speaking to countless clubs and organizations, offering advice about social media and marketing when I was an insurance agent. "There is better use of your time!" so I was told.

It took several months of consistently gifting and not expecting anything in return until I began to truly feel the effects of my efforts. And then it was as if a flood gate had opened up. People were emailing, Facebooking, and calling me to talk about insurance.

You may see it as a gamble, but you're in insurance, so you should be used to taking risks.

INSURANCE AS AN ARTIST

"How do I know what art to make? How do I know what gifts to give? This is the crux of it. Once you commit to being an artist, the question is an obvious one. The answer is the secret to your success. You must make a map. Not someone else. You."
— An excerpt from Seth Godin's NY Times Bestseller
  Linchpin: Are You Indispensible?

Without art there is only commodity. Transaction. Data. No one is changed in the process. No one is inspired. *You* get shopped. *You* lose the account. *Your* fault.

To be an artist means you are creating, sharing and gifting. The old capitalist mindset of hoarding and keeping an idea for fear that if a competitor finds out he or she will take it and get credit for it is pathetic. It devalues what you do. It devalues *you*. The artist simply shares.

To be clear – there is a difference between a *gift* and *art*. Think *matter* and *form*, or *element* and *word*. A gift is a tangible item or experience you offer. Your art is the spirit behind the gift – it's what moves people. Your art changes people for the better. It inspires. Art can't be resold. It's *how* you do *what* you do. It is in how you create *an insurance experience!*

As insurance artists, our art can take on many forms:

As you can see, to be an artist requires offering more than the policy and service expectation levels that insureds have become accustomed to. Some of these may look really simple to do, but do you do them? Being an artist is not easy, it requires a particular frame of mind focused on giving. Whether it is giving of your attention, or giving of your creativity.

Keep in mind there is no *how-to* on becoming an *artist*. It's something within you that you feel you must share. It's who you are. That's why *being* the right kind of person is so important. Having the right attitude is imperative for you to grasp the notion of gifting and becoming an artist. If you were hoping I was going to share a step-by-step for becoming an artist – I cannot. I can only share what other insurance artists are doing (as in the previous examples).

Just begin by doing some selfless acts and study how you feel afterwards. You will find that one-sided generosity causes you to immediately feel a swelling of goodness inside you that you want to reproduce often. The cool part is that you begin to give more and more. That level of giving sparks a cycle of gifting that will have a dramatic impact on your market (you will never know how far your selfless efforts reach).

I agree with Ed Lamont (www.lamontconsultinggroup.com) 100% – the enemy of the insurance agent today is **SAMENESS**. We all act and look the same. We take ACORD apps out on appointments (or worse yet, yellow legal pads); we use the same proposal forms; we use the same big words like "aggregate" and "liability"; and our business cards are all stupid...

This industry we are in is a great opportunity to capitalize on the platform we have been given to showcase our artistic ability. The thing about art is that it changes people for the better. Ironically, we don't pay for the changing effect of the art; instead, we pay for the transaction portion – the product (like the CD or an iTunes song; a painting or a book, etc.).

My clients pay premiums to the company I place them with. I earn a commission from the company for this. But what my clients experience throughout our relationship, I call that 'The Insurance Xperience'. It's my art.

Not only do I protect my clients' assets, lives and families, I create and share *value* with them consistently. I connect them with others for their own betterment. I don't expect anything in return, and yet, I know I'm worth much more than the commission I earn each year on their policy. I ensure that they know they are getting their dollar's worth and then some. They can't really put a price on what I do. Art causes people to talk and share with others the experience you create for them. It touches many people – and you, the artist, have no idea how far that circle will reach.

Artists who connect with their clients the best seem to go from unknown to rock star status overnight; but the truth is, these artists have been giving of themselves for years and years... it only appears they are an overnight sensation. The value they have been putting out in this world has been slowly attracting the counterpart of the value – in our case, the client who WANTS to do business with us.

The purpose of this section is to help you discover the artist within yourself and begin gifting your art to your marketplace; and as a result attract people who want to buy.

Selling is much easier when the prospect wants to buy. So how do we attract people who will want to buy from us?

8 | **The Hybrid Model**

"Sometimes you have to be willing to be misunderstood."

– Jeff Bezos,
CEO of Amazon.com

This is where you, as the Young Insurance Professional, create a *value difference* between yourself and every other agent in your market.

PART 1 OF HYBRID MODEL | YOUR PERSONAL BRAND

A distinct personal brand is necessary in this industry. Otherwise, you are going to look like everybody else. Do you want to get treated like a QUOTE? Or, would you rather be treated like a respected professional? Would you rather chase after prospects? Or, would you rather have prospects calling you because of what they have heard?

We are going to highlight five areas where you can separate yourself from the competition and develop a personal brand that becomes talked about in your marketplace. Your competitors will hate you. Which is good. Your clients will rave about you to their friends. Which is great. And you will enjoy the peace of mind knowing that you are different and authentic.

#1 Voicemail

Let's talk about your voicemail for a minute. Am I such an idiot that I don't know what day of the week it is? If my time was valuable to you, you'd answer my freakin' call. And I completely understand that you're either away from your desk or on the other line.

Did your boss give you a mandate telling you to record your voicemail with these cliché lines? Or did you just assume you had to record them this way?

Rerecord your voicemail and have some fun PLEASE! Do us all a favor. If I get a lame voicemail, I will hang up as I begin to hear it and I know you do the same as well.

Your voicemail is a great tool that works while you are not present! Utilize it! Here are some examples of voicemail that will cause others to stop and think in terms of YOU.

Don't find fault, find a remedy; anybody can complain. That's a quote from Henry Ford. This is Matt Brown, Insurance Advisor with Hays Insurance, and I'm an expert at finding remedies, how can I best help you? I will return your call within twenty four hours, thank you and have an awesome day!

You have to 'Be' before you can 'Do' and 'Do' before you can 'Have'. One of Zig Ziglar's insights. This is Matt Brown, Insurance Advisor with Hays Insurance, what can I 'Do' for you today? I will return your call within 1 business day.

We don't like their sound, and guitar music is on its way out. Decca Recording Company stated that when they rejected the Beatles in 1962. This is Matt Brown with Hays Insurance, I won't reject any of your ideas so please share after the tone and I will return your call within 24 hours.

*Hi! You've reached the voicemail for Matt Brown, Insurance Advisor with Hays Insurance. I'm under several deadlines at this time and email may be an easier way for us to connect. My email address is **matt@haysinsurance.net**. Otherwise, please leave me a message and I will return your call within 24 hours.*

Details to consider for your voicemail strategy:

→ Be thought-provoking, use quotes that are not cliché and used every day

→ Be fun – it may help if you are standing when you record your voicemail... and smile!

→ Consider using an insurance statistic with a thought-provoking statement or question
→ Direct callers to your email (this trains people to respect your time)
→ Message should be no longer than 15-20 seconds
→ Change voicemail on a daily basis to be ultimately effective

In a hilarious Seinfeld episode, George Costanza is screening his phone calls to hide from his ex-girlfriend. George actually sings a personalized version of the Greatest American Hero theme song (a classic from the 80s): "Believe it or not, George isn't at home. Please leave a message at the beep!" You can find this on YouTube and I highly recommend you watch it for the inspirational value. Here is a link (may not be valid after a while):
http://www.youtube.com/watch?v=caoYdiq3kak

For your own message, you can pick the theme song from one of your favorite shows or a classic show that will help connect to your client base.

#2 Business Card

I love Gitomer's business card exchange bit he does during his seminars. He tells everyone to exchange one of their cards with someone sitting next to them. Then he tells them to look long and hard at the card. He then states, "If the card is a piece of crap, I want you to rip it in half." This card is part of their image! Most cards are lame and typically find their way to some form of trash can.

My goal is that my card makes it next to your computer monitor. In fact, when I went in to do a final presentation to the CEO of Interactive Robotics (**interactive-robotics.com**), I noticed that my business card was on his keyboard standing up.

I knew I had made an impression and got a boost of confidence before making my presentation. After accepting a signed check and application from Johnathan, I asked him if I could take a picture of my business card on his keyboard – I told him that was why I got those cards, because they earn key real estate within an office (like next to a monitor).

A good card (probably 1 out of 500) is not only kept, but SHARED with others. The rest go in some kind of trash can. A couple other ideas I have come across include – a financial advisor takes his corporate business card and sticks two stamps on the back; one was a $.33 stamp from 2000, and the other is a $.44 stamp from 2011. He laminates the cards and intends to cause others to stop and think about how he may be able to help them grow their investment over time.

And that's the objective – to get people to *stop* and *think*.

#3 Name Tag

> *"Authentic expression of your personal truth is a risk.*
> *Take it. Comfort zones are overrated."*
> — Scott Ginsberg, The Nametag Guy
> (www.hellomynameisscott.com)

Ever hear of Scott Ginsberg? He has been wearing a name tag since November 2007... everyday. He has become a globally recognized authority on initial engagement strategies with others. Yep. He wears a name tag with his name "Scott" everyday... everywhere he goes. People are just naturally encouraged to approach him and introduce themselves. It's amazing.

Scott is so serious that he wears a name tag on each layer of clothing in case he takes off one. He even has it tattooed on his chest. You read that right. That's commitment to the cause.

I'm not suggesting you tattoo a name tag to your chest, but I am asking you to think about what would happen if you created your own name tags and wore them at select times. Networking events or anywhere you would be around people who may not know you. And have fun with it.

For instance, I created several slide-ins to fit a name badge that goes around my neck. Depending on my mood and the occasion, I insert one of the following:

Risk Doctor

Ask Me for an Idea

@mattmbrown

"Do you have protection?"

I have worn these to pretty much any event you can think of. Many people will just look at me weird, but you know they want to ask, "What's up with the name tag?" I don't care though, I just like making people think about me. Of course, many will approach me and ask me about my name badge.

It's a great conversation starter. Usually the conversations begin with a good laugh – which takes pressure off situations that are normally fixed with anxiety and nervousness to begin with. I've never been punched in the face for wearing my name tag – I guess I consider that to be the *worst case scenario*. So in case you were worried about getting punched in the face for wearing a name tag to places untypical, I've never had that happen to me.

#4 Email Signature

Often overlooked. Here is an example of mine, I have experimented over the past two years and this has received the best feedback to date.

Matt Brown

The Insurance Producer

The Insurance Agent for People Who Want To Produce More

C (419) 371-7053

BLOG www.mattmbrown.com

LINKEDIN www.linkedin.com/in/matthewmbrown

YOUTUBE Matt Brown TV

TWITTER @mattmbrown

VALUE NOTICE: Matt's definite purpose in life is to challenge the status quo and gift his energy, creativity, and expertise to the marketplace ultimately helping others stop, think, consider and become better. His mission is to create a unique insurance experience for his clients that turns them into raving fans. He does this by solving their insurance problems; sharing ideas that help them produce and profit more; providing consistent value over the course of their relationship; and responding quickly with solutions... and he has fun, everyday.

Let's break it down:

→ My name is actually a *hyperlink* to my website

→ My *title* is part of my brand, what's your personal brand?

→ My *tagline*. This is also part of my brand. I'm the insurance agent for people who want to produce more. I network with businessowners, professionals and executives on a very regular basis and value to these kinds of people means anything that will help them "produce more". So this is really just more of my personal brand.

→ Cell phone – simple.

→ Blog – again, my website URL

→ Linkedin Profile

→ YouTube Channel

→ Twitter handle

→ Confidentiality Notice – I used to have a confidentiality notice at the bottom of my email. I copied and pasted it from someone else's. Then I realized that everyone had one and they were really annoying and would sometimes lead to an extra page when printed. So I decided I would utilize this space for a *Value Notice*. It's my Major Definite Purpose and Personal Mission Statement. It's size 8 font and anyone who actually catches it and realizes it is NOT a confidentiality notice will be pleasantly surprised. I know when other agents on committees for Chamber and so forth see my email they think, "Oh c'mon Brown, are you serious?!" That's great. I take great comfort in that.

So, create your own signature that will be fun and social. This signature works while you are not present. Another great way to leverage inbox real estate.

#5 Personal Appearance

"Now, you're telling me you were so ingrained with white trash DNA, your facial hair actually grows in on its own all white trashy like that?"
— Dennis Miller as Zander Kelly in the movie *Joe Dirt*

Our profession, if we want to be taken seriously, requires us to look professional.

Let's address the basics:

1. Many young insurance professionals claim that they live in a market or community that would be offended by someone who dresses up and looks all *fancy shmancy*. I don't buy it. That's an excuse because you simply don't like to wear a tie. Just admit it so we can move forward. I've never had anyone roll their eyes at me in disgust for wearing French Press shirts with cuff links. If anything, it emits success and people tend to respect you more because it's obvious you respect yourself.

2. Shaving and grooming facial hair <u>every day</u> (I'm speaking to the male agents... I hope). Shaving everyday is imperative in my personal opinion. If you are going to grow a beard or goatee – it should look good on you and be tight and clean. If you look like a loser with a beard, don't grow it.

3. Your shoes should be like mirrors every day.

4. Press your shirts. Wrinkles are horrible on dress shirts. If you don't own an iron or know how to (wow...), then try hanging up your shirt in the bathroom when you shower. Shut the door to the bathroom and let the steam from your shower help de-wrinkle the shirt.

5. Smoking. I quit smoking in January 2010. It has been the best thing for my clothes and car (not to mention my health). The smell of smoke is nasty. Even if the contractor you are going to go see is nicknamed 'Smoky,' don't smoke on your way to the appointment. Bottom line, it's bad for your health and even worse for first impressions.

Summary

Your personal brand should reflect your attitude and personal beliefs. By holding back on personal enthusiasm you will become bland and just like every other agent in your market. If you are afraid that your Principal or Sales Manager will not embrace the 'new' you and your personal brand, look at it like this:

You start dressing sharper. Smelling better. You're clean shaven or have a well-manicured jaw line. Your voicemail is thought-provoking and fun. Your agency-issued business cards have a handwritten quote on the back. Your email signature reflects that of a market leader. As a consequence, you start connecting with more qualified prospects who enjoy your style and personal brand. Which also leads to more sales. What were you worried about again? Exactly.

PART 2 OF HYBRID MODEL | NETWORKING LIKE A PRO

What are the most effective *techniques* for networking? Well, there is no "step-by-step" technique. I'm of the mindset that you should be networking 24/7 all year long. My goal is to make one new friend each day. So where would be the best places to network? That depends on who your ideal client is, and where you will find them.

Most networking events offer a few speakers, and in-between presentations they have a networking time. What I have noticed is that most people sit at their table and talk with the people at their table. I've done this. But I do this because I choose to sit with people I don't yet know.

Many times, you see the same people sitting together and it's used as another opportunity to simply sit and chat on a Friday morning. Wrong idea. I go and I sit with complete strangers... or better yet, I find the table where my target connection is seated.

If I want to meet someone, there is no simpler route than to go and introduce yourself. The BEST route, actually, would be to have a mutual connection introduce you to your target connection; beef you up in a sentence or two, and then let you take it from there.

I have read several books on networking and many advocate having a 30 second *pitch*. I did this until one time I was asked straight up – "what's your pitch?" I was kind of pissed. I don't have a "pitch" ...or did I? I reviewed my 30 second commercial and it sounded great – but that's just it, it sounded like a commercial.

I believe in being brief with a sentence that encompasses what something does – like iTunes, "1000 songs in your pocket." That's genius. It tells me what it does in terms that relate to me. With insurance, it's a bit different. My pitch was something like this, "Hi, my name is Matt Brown and I help business owners and professionals protect their assets and investments."

Lame. I had variations of course. But they were lame too because I would run into other insurance agents who had similar variations. Don't get me wrong, I've heard worse lines than this – on the golf course (where I don't talk details about business) one time I heard a fellow agent ask one of the four in our group, "How's that homeowners insurance?" He said it half jokingly, but let's be honest – he was *still* serious.

What I do now is so much simpler and it's not about a pitch. I ask questions and listen. I personally like to learn about the other person first, depending on the event and the community it's in, because my network may be really strong there. I lead with questions like, "What is it that you do?" And then I listen.

I'll use this information for several reasons:

1. They tell me what they do and from that I can determine if they are someone I would INITIALLY be interested in connecting with for my selfish insurance purposes.

2. Or, I can determine what kind of connections they MAY be interested in connecting with and start to compile a mental list of potential "friends" I could introduce them to.

I may have to steer the conversation to get more details so I'll ask something like, "I see, what's the most frustrating part about the job?" This depends all on where the conversation has gone at this point. If I ask this it's because I want to know what kind of problem I may be able to help them fix (and many times, insurance is not the thing that comes to most people's minds).

They could respond in several ways, but the point is that I'm trying to connect and better understand this person's frustration. I'm not in a hurry to talk about me yet. And I'm definitely not trying to understand what kind of "type" this person is. Some sales training will have you trying to identify what it means when a prospect looks up or down, to the right, and everywhere else. It's too much work and I don't see how it could possibly be effective. My goal is to harmonize with the other person and make friends. That's it.

At some point in this conversation, the other party will ask me, "So what is it that you do?" This is where I ask a POWER QUESTION. Yes, I answer questions with a question. It's how I do what I do. But it works well. Power questions are questions that make the other party stop, think and consider something in terms of YOU.

Jeffrey Gitomer tells us that we should have 25 of these prepared in advance and depending on the prospect and what we know about them we can pick one to leverage with. Here are 5 great power questions: (What? You thought I was going to give you 25? Do some work for yourself!)

→ *What is it about your business' property and liability insurance plan that you like best?* (Hopefully in our conversation beforehand I had found out if he/she owned a business, owned the property, etc)

→ *If I could give you a magic wand to fix any problems with your current protection plan for the business, what would you fix?*

→ *What do you hate most about insurance?*

→ *How many times in the past year has your insurance agent shared an idea with you that helped you produce or profit more?* (I follow this with a free idea for improving their personal productivity. Most of my prospects are professionals or business owners. These people never have enough time. So I help them find more of it by sharing a technique with them. Then I follow that idea up with, "I share an idea each week with my clients. I would be happy to put you on my ezine list, it's not spam, just value."

→ *Cost aside, what's important to you about your business' insurance protection?*

So, here are my **_top 5 goals_** at any networking event:

1. Make friends
2. Determine how I can best help each new friend
3. Qualify friends for insurance purposes
4. Get permission from each new friend to put them on my ezine list
5. For *qualified insurance* new friends, ask for a follow up appointment to determine if I would be able to help them fix insurance problems

That's it. Did you see, *"Make a sale"* anywhere in that list? Nope. I'm not trying to make a sale when I'm networking. So why would I be nervous? I'm just trying to make new friends. I will admit, if you're not likeable in the first place – then you don't stand much of a chance. You probably shouldn't have gotten into sales. Being likeable is everything. It leads to trusting. Which leads to appointments. Which leads to sales.

Where Should I Be Networking?

Like I mentioned earlier, I network everywhere. But if it's not a 'true' networking event, I dial down the power questions.

I don't try to enlist people on my ezine list in social settings. I just make friends and my goal is to be the most authentic person they have had a conversation with in a very long time. If they ask me what I do, I tell them, "I'm in insurance. Mostly commercial business, but I have markets for auto, home (life, health, umbrella, boat, RV, etc)."

If they're interested, they usually chime back, "Oh really! I should have you quote my stuff." This is where I draw the line in the sand for them by saying, "I would love to. But quoting implies I work for free, and I can't afford to do that. I earn a living by solving problems. So maybe we can talk for a few minutes next week, review what you've got right now, and if I think I can help, I'll tell you so. If I can't help, I'll tell you that too. I just don't want to waste your time, or my own. Sound cool?"

Sometimes people respond, "Oh, I just thought I'd see if you could save me some money." This allows me the opportunity to separate myself from every other agent. You may initially see this as a lost opportunity to gain a new client, but I say _make your mark_. I will even typically try to tell prospects that I'm probably not going to save them any money.

Depending on your niche and target client, you might plan your lifestyle and frequented locations. Are you trendy? Maybe you should stick around Starbucks for 10 minutes each morning and make friends. Are you athletic? Maybe you should join a gym and take classes where you will make other like-minded friends. Are you all about business development in your community? Chamber is the answer.

If your chamber is small, get involved and offer to take a leadership role to make positive change happen. You won't get paid for your efforts, but you will create a name for yourself and attract people.

Also, sites like **www.meetup.com** connect groups of people with similar interests around your community. You may have to travel 30-45 minutes to meet up with these new groups of people. But after several meetings have passed and your likeability and trust factors have been established, you will begin to have people approach you. Your career as a young insurance professional must be taken seriously by YOU. If you don't take it seriously, no one else will either.

How to Become the *Ultimate* Connector!

I recommend you begin building your network and keep all business cards in a box. Write key notes on the back of cards about the other person – like what their main problems are that need fixing (maybe not insurance related). When you come across a solution person for them, or someone that you feel would help strengthen their network, connect them. This not only helps them, but it makes you look like a pro networker and someone to be viewed as *leader*. I use email as a tool to increase notoriety and respect, as well as becoming the *ultimate* connector in my market.

Scenario

One of my clients has a business built on innovation – they help you take your idea for a product and manifest it into the real thing. As I was meeting with a new connection over coffee she told me about an idea she had for a cutting table. She has years and years of restaurant experience (as an owner and Chef), and had an idea for creating a cutting table that is functional and comfortable for those cooking in restaurants. I told her about my client who helps people do exactly what she wants to do, and that I would introduce them via email. She was ecstatic!

Here's how you should proceed with any email introduction:

1 | Put both party's emails in the "To:" section. Do not "CC" or "BCC" either of them, because it is going to both of them!

2 | The "Subject Line" should read, "Introductions to Connect!" or "Johnathan meet Alisa... Alisa meet Johnathan!"

3 | The body of your message reads like this:

Alisa,

I am so glad we got the opportunity to connect this morning! I can't wait to see what happens with your genius product idea!

Per our conversation, I would like to introduce you to Johnathan Rankin, CEO and President of Interactive Robotics, LLC here in Ada, Ohio. Johnathan began the business in 2009 after graduating from Ohio Northern University with a BS in Advanced Manufacturing and Design Analysis. His business works as a consulting service that utilizes technologies such as CADD (Computer Aided Drafting and Design) for developing robotics that help streamline work processes for clients of all shapes and sizes. Johnathan is also an Adjunct Professor at Rhodes State College in his "spare time."

To learn more about Johnathan, check out his Linkedin profile at

linkedin.com/pub/johnathan-rankin/16/b44/56b

Johnathan has all of the resources, connections and tools to take any idea you have and manifest it into a product with avenues for sales and marketing success of it.

Johnathan,

Alisa McPheron is a local celebrity, chef, entrepreneur, and a thought-leader. She has so many connections it's ridiculous. We got talking this morning and she mentioned that she had a product idea that could revolutionize the culinary industry. I told her you would reach out to her after I introduced the two of you via email. Please be sure to do so at your earliest convenience!

I'm confident you will both hit it off great; I'm really stoked about everything happening around us right now. Talk to you both soon!

My best,

Matt Brown
The Insurance Producer

Notice the following regarding the email introduction:

A | First name basis – be friendly.

B | Revisit the passionate conversation you had with Alisa and highlight the main point for this follow up.

C | Introduce the other party, in this case, Johnathan. Use his Linkedin profile for gathering the specific details that you will use to share as part of a quick snapshot of the individual and their business. Also include their Linkedin URL so that Alisa can find out more information about them if she likes.

D | Use a closing sentence for introducing Johnathan; this can be used for almost all introductions (assuming the person is marginally connected at best).

E | Introduce 1st party to the 2nd party now – in this case, now it's Alisa's turn to meet Johnathan

F | Same idea as before, give a Reader's Digest snapshot of who they are and what they need help with. (In this instance, Alisa did not have a Linkedin profile so I simply used all of the information I gathered in our initial meeting; this requires you to ask good questions so you can show that you were truly listening).

G | Always encourage the person who can do the helping to reach out first. This gives them the ball and allows them to touch base first.

H | End on a positive note. Get excited about the opportunity that sits before both of them.

In summary, connecting others via email is beneficial for you because:

→ It's a way to give value first and thus activate the law of attraction in your life

→ It's a great way to feel great about yourself!

→ It's an excellent way to showcase yourself as a *Connector*

→ It's an even better way to show both parties that you are concerned about their best interests and want only the best for them

→ It's crucial for showcasing yourself as someone who listens, pays attention to detail, and is a leader

→ It's a selfless act, the world needs more of these kinds of actions taking place, so just do it

Connecting others is vital for business success, but more importantly, it's vital for your personal growth as an individual and for separating yourself from the other producers in your market. Become a *Connector* and help others succeed first!

PART 3 OF HYBRID MODEL | IDENTIFYING AND CONNECTING WITH *YOUR* TRIBE

I want you to consider where you live for a moment. Whether you live in a large metropolis or small village, there is a common factor – people long *to belong*. In many cases, it is the community that pulls together after a tragedy and helps one another. I saw this first hand when my brother-in-law was killed in Afghanistan in February 2011. People you haven't spoken to in over 10 years came out to offer hugs and tears for the fallen member of the community. It is an impressive sight and an overwhelming experience for all members to witness people coming together. Social networking sites connect us so we can keep up on everyone's lives but *real* engagement is when we connect in person.

I will take it one step further and deeper. I view communities as modern day tribes. Tribes, historically speaking, were smaller in scope but we can learn from them. In the Bible, there is a law against usury (charging high interest) within the tribe. People did not charge interest on loans that were given amongst members of the tribe, because it was thought to push people apart. It was perfectly cool to charge interest to anyone outside the tribe. Can you imagine, however, posing that argument with your banker in your community? That would be hilarious.

I have discovered that by giving freely of my talents and expertise to my tribe I have been able to gain much of what I wanted in return. The community portion of this hybrid model is your charitable arm. It's you, using your gifts and talents, to positively impact your community. What can you give? Where can you give it?

Anyone can volunteer at the local soup kitchen... but what if you could share some ideas with the Director on how they could better market themselves to obtain more donations? Or an idea to help streamline a process that helps the kitchen perform at a more productive level – reaching more people in shorter time.

As we have learned, in this new economy – the gift economy – your status is according to how much you give. And the best gifts are ideas that help others **produce** and **profit more**. If you are volunteering in your community with the hidden motive of making more insurance sales, that's the wrong game plan. People are too transparent – I can tell when someone is in a club or volunteering simply for the sake of getting something in return. Go and give freely, expect nothing, and reap everything. Sales? Eventually, yes, of course. But more valuable than that is your reputation. Become known as a go-*giver*.

Some more examples of what you could do:

→ Church related opportunities (Habitat for Humanity, Soup Kitchen, etc.)

→ Chamber – join the Small Business Development Committee (or create one) and offer to speak on a subject where you have some expertise that would help others in business produce or profit more, ultimately benefiting the tribe

→ Join a local club like Rotary, Lions, Optimists, United Way, etc.

→ Take a leadership role, chair a committee

→ Create your own community benefit opportunity

→ Find a cause that needs attention and recruit others to join you in your efforts to offer specific solutions via projects, etc.

PART 4 OF HYBRID MODEL | SPEAK AND WRITE YOUR WAY TO THE TOP OF YOUR MARKET

Public Speaking

"According to most studies, people's number one fear is public speaking. Number two is death. Death is number two. Does that sound right? This means to the average person, if you go to a funeral, you're better off in the casket than doing the eulogy."
— Jerry Seinfeld, Comedian

I have noticed that the top 10% of money earners in this industry have one thing in common – a great ability to speak to an audience or group.

When you can speak with confidence and engage others in an audience by sharing valuable content and a little humor, doors open up. For some reason, we as people believe that a great speaker is someone who is naturally smarter and more talented than those who don't speak. That may not be true, but we believe it to be so.

I was terrified of speaking so I immediately joined Toastmasters, a public speaking group that offers step-by-step training for getting you more comfortable talking in front of others. The group I was in was small, maybe 5 or 6 members total. We met at 6:00 a.m. on the 1st and 3rd Wednesday of each month.

I remember my first speech clearly, I forgot my material and completely froze... in front of only two members in the audience. The great thing about Toastmasters is that your fellow members are there to support and encourage you. It's like, you write a speech based on the outline and topic you are given, and then you share it with a group of friends. There is no reason to be afraid of the group not accepting your ideas, they are there to support and encourage! The purpose of joining Toastmasters is to learn how to overcome your own internalized fear of speaking in front of a group of people.

Public speaking is one of the most terrifying things to do, there is no doubt; however, I have learned that the more prepared you are, the easier it is to speak to a group. When you know your material *inside and out*, it becomes easier to address others. When you have to use cards or notes, it can be a bit nerve-racking because you don't want to forget something.

Also, once I realized that the people in the audience <u>want</u> you to succeed and deliver an awesome presentation or speech, it made it a lot easier to do.

The "little me" would always tell the "big me" that my ideas would be rejected and I would be laughed off the stage. Why would anyone in an audience want you to fail? That means they would have to sit through a horrible talk, and they don't want to do that! They want to be entertained and educated. I also heard a quote once that went something like this, "If you knew who stood beside you, you would feel no fear." Reading that was like an "Aha" moment for me. I realized that God gave me a gift and my job was to deliver it in the most creative and engaging way possible, why would He let me fail?

Let's learn how we can become a better speaker and a few techniques for delivering the presentation of a lifetime!

The Skill Set for Speaking

There are plenty of people who talk just to be heard – annoying. The best speakers are those who can influence and persuade their audience to take action.

Your focus, as a speaker, is to move your audience; they should think, feel and act differently afterwards. Great speaking skills are learned and, according to Albert Mehrabian of UCLA, there are three main components to the message you will deliver to an audience.

1 | **The Words**
     7% of what you actually say is conveyed to the audience. The words are important and must be chosen carefully, but remember that lame speaker who used all the big words and put you to sleep? Exactly.

2 | **The Tone**
     38% of your message is conveyed through your tone and emphasis on particular words. Remember, it's not what you say so much as how you say it.

3 | **The Body**
     55% of your message is conveyed in your body. This is because there are 22 times as many nerves from the eye to the brain as from the ear to the brain. Why do you think great comedians use so many visual impressions as part of their bit?

During Your Presentation

"Slow down, pause and smile between points and sentences."
— Brian Tracy

Don't get caught up in your body gestures so much that you lose focus of why you are speaking in the first place! If you are trying so hard to remember how you should have your hands or where you shouldn't stand, or whatever, you will begin to lose momentum in your talk. Lou Holtz once noted that public speaking is simply about you getting on stage in front of other people and sharing ideas that help them. That's it. Don't be overly concerned about all of the details. Know your material and practice, you will be fine.

Putting Your Presentation Together

Use a basic three-part structure for developing your speech. This works great for any speech you must give that lasts 1-30 minutes.

Part 1 | The Opening

Tell the audience what you are going to talk about, give them an idea of where you are going with your talk. For example, "Thank you for being here. In the next few minutes, I want to share with you three strategies you can leverage as part of your own speech and presentation that will truly engage your audience."

Part 2 | Deliver What You Promised

This is where you share what you told the audience you were going to share in the opening. Any speech you give that is under 30 minutes should have three main points (at most).

For example, "The opening of your speech, delivering what you promised in the opening and your summary are vital to the success of your presentation. Let's look at each of these in order."

Part 3 | Sum It Up

No one is going to remember everything you talked about. Drive home one final part that encompasses the message and has some sort of call to action. You can build it by repeating some of the main points you made earlier, or just cut to the heart of it all.

For example, I once had to give a 4 minute speech to nearly 1,500 individuals attending an Upward Sports event; kids, parents, grandparents, etc.

My summary sounded like this, "At the end of the day, the only thing that truly matters is the decision to _do_ and to act upon that decision immediately. That's your moment, and you only get so many. So, simply, _do_."

5 Tips For How to Reduce Nervousness

Before every presentation or speech I give, I get nervous. I'm less nervous than I used to be, but I still get butterflies. Here are some techniques that I learned from reading Brian Tracy's _Speak to Win_ that have helped me reduce my nervousness before a talk or presentation:

→   Go to the room where you will be speaking the day before and just sit in it. Take a picture. Stand where you will be standing to deliver your speech. Envision the room packed. Practice walking where you will walk throughout your speech. If possible, run through your speech to the empty room and deliver a great speech (even though no one is there).

→   Pump yourself up before you go up to speak by saying to yourself, "This is a great talk! I can hardly wait! This audience is going to be blown away!" On the car ride over to the speech, simply repeat over and over again, "I like myself! I like myself! I like myself!" This actually does make you feel comfortable and at ease.

→   Wiggle your toes – I didn't actually think this would work but it does. Tracy states it is correlated with our childlike tendencies that we wiggled our toes when we were excited as youngsters; reproduce the feeling by wiggling them before speaking.

→ Roll your shoulders – this is where you store tons of tension.

→ Be grateful for the opportunity to share with an audience. It's a privilege to be permitted to stand in front of an audience and share ideas that help them in one way or another. Even if it is a "boring" subject, you can deliver it in such a way that people are moved. Be thankful and grateful for that opportunity to connect.

Final Thoughts

Ever watch comedians take the stage? Or any great speaker for that matter? They walk confidently and quickly to the mic. Also, if someone is introducing you, walk confidently and quickly towards them (smiling) and shake their hand (or hug it up if you feel it's appropriate).

Turn and face the audience, if you're not already! Use silence to settle everyone. I will just look at people and smile... not for too long, I don't want to freak them out or anything, but you have to gain their attention through silence momentarily.

Your opening statement should be confident, clear, friendly, interesting, thought-provoking, attention-grabbing, and fun. That's a whole lot of something in one opening statement, but it's possible. Be creative. Your opening bit is huge! I like humor in the form of a question, typically. The key is connecting your opening statement with your closing thoughts – not easy to do, but it will show the audience that you have done your work.

Remember, people make a personal assessment of you based on how you look (what you are wearing, etc) within the first 30 seconds. Nothing should be overly distracting, otherwise, it will take away from your message and your likeability will decrease. If it's part of your personal brand, then by all means go ahead with it.

My personal rule of thumb is to dress in a way that the audience will respect me because it is apparent that I respect myself by the way I dress. I want to be taken seriously when I have everyone's attention.

In the end, just be yourself when you are speaking. Be authentic and genuine. Don't try to talk all professionally because people don't listen. This one skill has been the difference between mediocrity and huge success for many people. It's one of the hardest skills to hone because it takes courage to stand up in front of a crowd and share yourself with them. But the individuals who are able to do this in the most authentic way possible are the ones who reap the most benefits.

7 Immediate Action Steps for Speaking Success!

1. Join a local Toastmasters organization. Just Google it.

2. Take a course at a local university or community college on public speaking.

3. Take a theatre/acting course – it will push you outside your comfort zone!

4. Read Brian Tracy's *Speak to Win: How To Present With Power in Any Situation*

5. Create a 20-30 minute presentation on something cool and interesting that local clubs and organizations would want to learn more about. I used social media as a topic to help me get in front of thousands of people locally in my markets. You could do the same.

6. Contact all local clubs or organizations in your market and tell them you are interested in speaking to their group (or at an upcoming event) on the subject of _____. Send them a one page outline of your presentation and ask them who you should be in contact with to make it happen. Examples of organizations you should find include, but are not limited to; Lions, Rotary, Optimists, local councils, boards, etc. Just ask your local chamber for a listing of organizations and presidents' names/emails.

7. Speak to a local university classroom. Professors are usually open to guest speakers, depending on how your message relates to their course.

The bottom line is simply <u>to speak</u>. Go and share a message wherever there are people willing to listen. I even practiced reading scriptures to our parishioners at church. Just standing up in front of others who are looking directly at you gets you facing your fear.

After delivering a great presentation, your chest should swell up with elation and excitement! That's a natural high. That's what I love about it. Go, therefore, *speak* and become known and rich in your market.

Writing

> *"The only way to learn how to write is to write and write and write and write and write and write and write."*
> — *Elbert Hubbard*

If you really want to be the market leader, start by writing. Get up early to read and write. Read something positive and write down your ideas surrounding it. Read something about sales or marketing, and write down a recap and your ideas surrounding what you read. Just write!

Over the course of time you will begin to develop your *person* and your brand. I write how I talk. That's how simple I keep it. When you read my book it should be like a conversation between you and me. Don't worry about conjugating of verbs and all this and that – just write from the heart.

The cost of failure for you, as a young insurance professional, has decreased significantly over the past five years. To cold call on 30 businesses in person and fail could cost you and your agency hundreds of dollars in time, energy, fuel expense and paper.

It's a necessary expense, but one that should be preplanned and carefully strategized. To fail in a blog post costs you nothing. To not have your Tweet re-Tweeted, costs nothing. To not have an eHow.com article you wrote not shared by readers on their Facebook costs you nothing. Writing is a medium that you can leverage to inspire and change the way people think. Good writing has power.

To get started:

1 | Fire up a blog!
    www.blogger.com
    www.blog.com
    www.wordpress.com
    www.typepad.com
    There's a lot of platforms out there to choose from– pick one you like and go with it.

2 | **www.YourName.com**
    Go to one of the following domain purchase sites and buy a **.com** with your name. Don't be a tightwad, they're $15 or less, you spend more on a night out anyways, and this is an investment for your future – assuming your name is not already taken. You can have this domain name be a "forwarder" to your free blog site. So now, on your social networks, business cards, and anywhere else, you will promote your blog as **www.yourname.com**. You also get one free email address forwarder with the purchase of a domain – so now you can also give out your personalized email as **yourname@yourname.com**. That looks a lot more professional than **yourname@gmail.com** or **your_name4562@yahoo.com**. Appear professional and you will be treated as such. Appear professional and you'll be treated as such. Here are two places where I've invested in dozens of domains: www.godaddy.com and www.domaininseconds.com.

3 | Start reading and writing on a consistent basis. _Consistent_ means one blog post per week. 500 words is a good rule of thumb in most cases... however, some of the best blogs now are 250 words or less and come out on a very frequent basis. One of the best bloggers in the business world is Seth Godin (**www.sethgodin.com**). Sign up for his as a great example of what to do.

Blogging is a great start. Your goal is to refine your skills in a public forum. By sharing your blog post on Facebook and Linkedin you get over the fear of sharing ideas. Your goal is to build up value in your tribe and community and set your sights on getting published in local publications and industry specific magazines.

Why? Let me ask you a question – do you think a prospect would rather see your boring business card or some white paper or article you wrote about your industry that is featured in an insurance magazine? That's value. I'd rather slap the magazine down on their desk with **my** article ear marked.

Even if they don't read it and tell you how awesome the article was, you're published. You did something that your competitors did not do. You aren't standing on the desk beating your chest about how cool you and your agency are, you are using other mediums to share that (like the magazine with your article published in it).

How To Get Published

This seems daunting but it can be done. I asked for some inside tips from Todd Boyer, Director of Corporate Communications and Public Relations at Ohio Mutual Insurance Group, here is what he shared with me:

"Depends which one [insurance magazine] and how you want to be portrayed. The most effective way is to draft a 600-1000 word piece on a current topic and send it, along with your professional qualifications (bio) to the publication's editor as a submission, with a cover letter.

"You're not likely to be paid anything, but the exposure and cache of being 'published' is generally more than enough value for the effort.

"The other approach is to identify a unique story idea and contact a writer at the publication, share the idea with them, and offer to be an information resource for the article they might write on the subject.

"You should expect to be working a minimum of 4 months before publication date, so if your story ideas have any time/seasonal elements, you'll need to keep that in mind."

Another great way to increase notoriety within the industry and showcase yourself on your social networks, etc, is to get involved with PIA (**www.pianet.com**) or The Big

"I" (**www.iiaba.net**). These organizations are awesome for connecting you with all the right resources, tools and people you need in order to succeed and develop.

Cultivate a great relationship from the very beginning and keep in touch with many in your state's organization. Connect with them on Facebook, Linkedin, Twitter, everywhere. You want them to be able to see how you are separating yourself from your colleagues.

Eventually, they will reach out to you for some perspective and possibly a feature in their monthly magazine. That's what happened to me. I had developed great rapport and relationships with our companies who were contributors and members of PIA Ohio, and many leaders at these companies nominated me for PIA National's Young Insurance Professional of the Year in 2011.

This sparked more curiosity and PIA Ohio contacted me to write a feature about what I was doing that was separating me from everyone else around me. This was also at the same time I was finalizing this book and I was a couple months out from releasing it. I asked the Director of Communications if she would put my book's website in with the article, and she was thrilled to do so.

I saved thousands in advertising for a full page *value* ad. Not only that, it gave me a TON of credibility right off the rip with the feature article on me. I wouldn't lie to you – writing has led me to everything.

How to Become a Local Celebrity

Another great way to get in front of your community is to find free publications in your market that are at practically every store. Find the Publisher/Editor and ask them if you could submit an article to their paper.

Depending on the theme of the publication, you could find your niche market and ideal clients through this and be gifting a value message each month/quarter in the form of an article. This is huge!

I have been a contributing monthly columnist with Full Heart Family News, located in Wapakoneta, Ohio but covering West Central Ohio – over 10,000 readers. I get cards in the mail each month from people telling me they appreciate my articles. It's flattering, but more importantly it's creating local celebrity status for me.

I would make it a priority to get involved with a well-known and respected organization in your market and begin creating a positive change. Anything you can do to lead an effort that will benefit the community and draw attention to the project is GREAT.

It's especially great if you chair the committee and are leading the project. That means local print and digital media will want to talk to you – and if they aren't calling you, you should be calling them and telling them what you are working on and ask them if they would want to do a story on it. All that really matters is that you get your picture in the paper. When your picture is in the paper for something positive in the community your name just increased in value.

People who tell you, "It's all in who you know," are full of *it*. All that truly matters is **who knows you** – and what they are saying about you behind your back. Hopefully you are giving them a reason to talk positively about you.

PART 5 OF HYBRID MODEL | HOW TO DOUBLE YOUR SALES, IMPROVE YOUR CLOSING RATIO, AND LOWER YOUR COST OF CLIENT ACQUISITION WITH AN EZINE

A *Value Ezine* is an email with content that helps the reader/subscriber producer or profit more immediately. It could include DIY (do it yourself) articles, how-to videos, tips, tricks, strategies, formulas, ideas, shortcuts, almost anything that is helpful for the subscriber.

How do you measure the return and benefits of email marketing? Simple, let's say that you use a paid service like *Constant Contact* (**www.constantcontact.com**) to create and share your ezine with 100 subscribers (current clients and anyone at networking events you have met and have said it was cool for you to put them on your list). The cost for the service is $30 per month for Constant Contact and you are allowed to have up to 2,000 email contacts at that cost (or you can get 500 email contacts for $15 per month). You can send as many emails as you want. Let's say you send one per week though (which should be the maximum).

Now, your agency may choose to spend $250 on a paid mass advertisement promoting you as their auto and homeowners specialist that results in 5 people walking into the agency. Out of the five who walked in:

→ One has an immediate need for auto insurance and you write them a policy for $1,000 annual premium

→ Three are potential future clients but after reviewing coverage with them you determine you can't help them at this time

→ One isn't interested at all in your agency, just popped in because they saw the ad

You sold an auto policy to the individual who had the immediate need. The policy was $1,000 annual premium; the average commission to be earned would be $150 (and then whatever cut you get since you're the producer). Since the agency spent $250 on the ad, the net cost to the agency was $100 ($250 ad - $150 commission). If you wanted to get more prospects into the store you could run another $250 ad and lose another $100, or you could...

...sell the $1,000 auto policy which nets $150 commission (minus your take as the producer). Despite being unable to offer competitive protection or solve any immediate problems for the three potential future clients, you made a favorable impression and obtained their email addresses and told them you would love to share your weekly value message with them – full of tips for DIY and How-to articles for home improvement and safety, etc. And screw the guy who came to the agency but was all about the dollars and wasn't interested in your ezine.

Now your agency doesn't have to spend another $250 on an ad because we will leverage the ezine with the four new subscribers (new client with the auto policy + 3 prospects you couldn't help at this time).

After two ezines being sent to the four new subscribers, one replies to the email and says that their daughter graduated from college and is looking for some renters insurance and that they told her you would call. You call her up and inquire about the renters policy.

During the conversation you also ask about her auto insurance. She said it was with the same company her parents were with but she was going to be getting off their plan now that she graduated from college. You told her you could combine her renters and auto and still get her an auto/home discount.

The end result is a $1,500 new business premium account in total, or a $225 commission. Now you have a PROFIT of $125 instead of a loss of $100 (minus the $15 per month cost of Constant Contact) for the ad your agency ran.

Impress Your Principal and Earn More Commission

Let's talk about the cost of acquisition (COA) for each client in your agency. Mock up your own chart based on the one below, ask your Principal if he or she has some time to discuss the advertising budget and efforts, and tell them you have some ideas that may cut expenses and increase sales at the same time.

Go ahead and plan on asking for a higher commission cut on any sale made via ezine acquisition as well, you've earned it.

When it comes to the cost of acquisition, all we mean is, "How much does the agency have to invest in a given medium for it to generate a new client?" The formula looks like this:

COA = Amount spent / The number of clients generated

Let's say you do direct mailing, it would look something like this:

$1,000 amount spent on 1,000 mailers (per year) / 10 number of clients generated (per year) = $100 COA

Start doing some investigating around your agency and find out where dollars are being invested for advertising and the number of clients generated per medium. Leave out email marketing for now since you don't have it in place yet. See the chart below as an example.

Type of Ad	Cost ($)	Clients	COA ($)
Newspaper	$10,000	50	$200
Direct Mail	$1,000	10	$100
Website	$5,000	20	$250
PWOMM	0	12	0

Don't start recommending the agency slash the budget based on these figures yet! Each lead (which we haven't looked at yet) is an opportunity based on the quantity and quality.

We are going to look at another chart that includes the leads generated *per source of advertisement* (and we will include email marketing now, too).

Type of Ad	Cost ($) / per yr	Clients	COA ($)	Leads
Newspaper	$10,000	50	$200	500
Direct Mail	$1,000	5	$200	15
Website	$5,000	20	$250	100
PWOMM	0	12	0	60
*Email Marketing	$360 (this price gets you up to 2,000 email contacts)	67	$5.37	0

* *Keep in mind, you acquired 67 clients from the sum total of 675 leads (from all other sources). This assumes that you can convert 10% of the total leads that contact your agency via all advertising sources.*

What I am proposing you do is share some information like this above with your Principal (if you don't already have an agency ezine). These figures are based on the AGENCY. Not you. If you're the producer then you probably aren't writing the business that walks in the door, you're supposed to be out "producing." But by showing the numbers above (tailored to your agency's specific budget and costs) you could build up a strong case for the agency purchasing a service like Constant Contact.

After reviewing the figures, suggest a one year trial of using the service. Tell your Principal the ezine could be a bi-monthly agency email to all leads received. He or she wouldn't really have to cut any of the budget because email marketing is so cheap anyhow.

Request that you may create your own email list for your leads and clients as well. Show your Principal what kind of "value" you will create and share with your audience. And, based on the COA, it makes sense to give something like this a shot. Personally, I went nearly 8 months in 2010 without cold calling, without mailings, without directly asking anyone about their insurance.

I simply went to local clubs in our markets and spoke on social media, and at the end of each presentation I would close talking about ezines and their value. I would ask everyone interested in subscribing to my weekly ezine simply pass a business card to the front. Each time I spoke I would get at least 20-40 cards. My database grew to over 250 in 6 months.

Every person on my email list is not a 100% quality lead, but the ones who are my ideal target clients (my niche) they *get* me and *like* me immediately. They read my ezine, I track where they are clicking in my ezine, and I watch as they email me about insurance. Law of Attraction at its finest.

As you will learn in the next chapter – it doesn't really matter how you are saying anything anymore... all that matters is what you are saying. People get tons of emails and they will skip over yours if the timing and content are not right. The next chapter is all about leveraging social media to engage others, apply these concepts to your ezine as well.

9 | The Social Way: Engagement in a *Social* Economy

"Connect. Create. Share. Inspire. Attract. That's social media in five words."

– Matt Brown

When I first got into the insurance industry in 2009, social media was just a few years deep and beginning to blow up everywhere. I saw it as an opportunity to grow my network exponentially by speaking to any service club, organization or group of people who would listen to me. I read a few books by "experts" in social media who were setting trends, and compiled all of their ideas into a philosophy of social media.

I preached that philosophy in my markets. I wasn't talking about insurance, which is not a sexy subject if you haven't realized that yet. But I was incorporating HOW I leveraged social media for ultimate engagement with my clients. I was selling a vision and helping my audiences better understand the WHY behind social media success.

I did not talk about "How to set up a Facebook Page for your business" or any other technical areas. I told audiences they could hire their 12, 13 or 14 year old to setup their Facebook Page, etc. My message was meant to help others transition into this new era and economy. It's hard for many of us to do because we are so programmed with industrialist and capitalist tendencies.

In the Industrial Age, the man who owned the machine made all the money. The man who worked on the machine was "secure" but needed it to earn a living and provide for his family. Now, <u>everyone</u> has access to THE machine. The machine is the $900 laptop and an internet connection. The tools include your brain, creativity and social media. So what *really* is *social media*?

Social Media | Defined

[soh-shul, mee-dee-uh\

-noun

1. Online **tools** that connect us and facilitate conversations

2. A means for **sharing** valuable content that **helps** others

3. A **platform**, an opportunity, and a **privilege**

There are many people who claim to be social media experts, but what is an *expert* really? And with something like social media, which is constantly changing and evolving, be leery of anyone claiming to be an official expert on the subject. I'll admit there are 'authorities' on the subject, but expert gets tossed around so much it has lost its value.

From the definition, we see key words have been enlarged and underlined. Social media is simply a means and a tool for creating conversations and engaging others. Social media is not about boosting sales. In fact, it's not about YOU at all.

THE SOCIAL EFFECT

"Local" is no longer confined by the city limit sign. This puts the client (or consumer in general) in control, where they rightly should be. It used to be that communities may have had only one insurance agency – and if that was you, you were assured the business of 90% of the community members, just because you were the only one they had access to.

Now the pyramid has flipped and the client is at the top. This means they can shop beyond their city limits. Of course they can go online, but that 15 minute insurance policy is <u>commodity</u>. You are more than that and can compete against lower prices based on your <u>value</u>.

However, your competition can be across town or even across the State and connect with someone who is right down the street from you. Word of mouth is now *world* of mouth. Being "local" is not as important as it used to be.

Of course dollars mean something, but most business owners remain loyal to a local shop because that person is in their business spending a lot of money each year. Personally, I can't afford to spend money in every business I represent. That's why I share ideas that help my clients produce and profit more.

With a well developed social strategy, we can create value differences that chip away at the competition's perceived value in the mind's eye of the client. I can create credibility, borrow trust from a prospect's friends on Facebook or Linkedin, share ideas that are helpful for my social community and as a result, even if I'm only twelve months into the business, I will get an opportunity to sit down with a big prospect. That's the power of social media – it increases perceived value.

The cost of failure is nil. The only thing you put in is time and this should be viewed as an investment. If you commit to consistency of value and keep your objective as "helping others" you will see a return on that investment.

When someone from your social community suggests your Page, or blog post, or video to someone outside of the tribe, that's called *Borrowed Trust*. You have been socially introduced (even though you may not be aware of it) to someone who is on the outside of your social community. They may choose to join yours as a result. This allows them to unobtrusively observe you.

If they like you, they may take the next step of signing up for your ezine. This is the next step that allows you to more personally engage your new community member. Eventually, they may choose to reply to your email or even call you to talk about insurance.

At this point, you have established rapport with them via your content; possibly even made a personal connection with them (depending on the content you have gifted); and as a result, their guard is down compared to you simply cold calling on them. This is part of what Gitomer means when he says *most salespeople aren't willing to do the hard work it takes to make selling easy.*

Social media is the **new cold call** and the true test of applying the Law of Attraction.

THE NOTION OF GIFTING AND BECOMING A *SOCIAL* ARTIST

It bothers me to hear agents say, "Well, they scratch our back so we'll scratch theirs, and that's just how we do business." Not me. I don't need you to scratch mine, but I'll scratch yours – no questions asked. I believe that my Maker is going to keep the gift cycle alive and I will have all that I want and need in this life because I am giving freely of what has been given to me.

You see, when you begin to tie this notion of gifting to social media's "liberation of content" you see that the world is posed for an evolution of heart, mind and soul. It's bigger than you thought. You really can have an impact at a global level from your very own office.

Viewing the privilege social media brings with it as a platform to do "art" is another gift in itself. Insurance has been viewed in the past as such a dry, boring industry. Let's give it color and passion. Social media and its tools have given you this platform to stand on and share from.

An insurance artist is the future of this industry. They change people for the better. They realize the importance for a human touch, amidst a digital era. Their art lasts long after the transaction. Their art gets shared, whether by a click of a button (in the form of a re-Tweet, etc.) or through word of mouth.

Social media is a platform for you to share your art. It is the privilege you are blessed with for creating a community based on value and substance. It is an opportunity for you to make a difference in the lives of countless others.

THE PRODUCTIVITY DEBATE

"But social media is a waste of time, I don't want my producers online Facebooking all day long." Common worry from your boss and rightly so.

Sixty minutes of planned, focused, social strategy is a good thing. Sixty minutes folks. It becomes a problem when we are consumed in the moment to check our notifications, wall feed updates and so on, only to be distracted from our *PG* Tasks for the day that are leading us towards ultimate success. But social media can in fact help you become MORE productive.

For example:

→ Eliminate watching the daily news (saves you at minimum 30 minutes) and instead "Like" pages that will PUSH information of importance to you (Insurance related pages, marketing pages, sales pages, social media update pages, etc). If you are prospecting restaurants for the 1st quarter, then you should "Like" all restaurant pages in your target market and keep up-to-date on what is going on in their life. Business news is important, but eliminate garbage that doesn't affect you or concern you.

The biggest problem you face, in regards to productivity, is when you poke the system and become consumed with *when* it will poke back. Social media is a medium for sharing your internalized dialogue with your social community.

That being said, it's also a very selfish platform in a sense. When you publish a blog article on your Facebook page you have made it public. Your mind goes into defensive mode and you feel the urge to check for feedback from your community. This can be very counterproductive, unless you have a plan.

A Good Plan

If you have a Facebook Page, set aside (batch) 1 hour per week to schedule all posts (can link to Linkedin and Twitter too) in advance. Utilize a social tool called Postling, found at **www.Postling.com**.

This tool allows you to schedule posts for any day or time during the week. You will also tell it when and where you would like to receive an update of any responses or activity on regarding your posts. You are able to receive a daily update of all notifications, sent directly to your email, which allows you to quickly and concisely check any activities on your networks and posts you shared.

THE SOCIAL FORMULA

Your Tribe

Define your target client. That sounds like part of your sales process, doesn't it? Niching it down is imperative. You need to clearly define the type of person you want to connect with. This person will walk, talk and act like you. This allows your voice to be heard and listened to. Sure, you will lose some potential clients because you are being genuinely YOU online (we will get into detail about what I mean here later), but the connection you will develop with those similar to you, who value your brand and what you offer, will be very strong.

My theory is — I want to do business with people like me. That's why almost all of my clients are entrepreneurs and professionals who are high-performers/non-conformists. They are the sales reps that 50% of the office loves while the other 50% hopes they die. They are the owners who try something that the critics scoff at. They are the entrepreneurs who are bootstrap operations and have failed miserably in the past, but they keep putting ideas into the world until eventually one sticks and becomes a success.

Think about it, the clients who are very much like you – how hard did you have to work to sell them a policy? You didn't *sell* them a policy; it was more like they <u>bought</u> it from you because they liked you. That's why I focus on sharing the kind of value that my ideal clients will be attracted to. I become a resource for them.

Storytelling

The best brands leveraging social media are sharing stories. Stories include testimonials from current clients who love you; or your agency/team members' story. Let's consider testimonials for a second...

First, you have to earn a testimonial. You don't earn a testimonial the day after you wrote the policy. Wait three months and shoot the client an email; it should sound something like this:

Susan,

I know we have only been in business together for a few months now, but I hope that my value has shown through already. [Hopefully you have shared a few ideas that have helped Susan produce or profit more, or sent a couple referrals her way]. Because you are someone I greatly admire and respect, I would be honored if you would be willing to offer a testimonial of my work up to this point. Please let me know a convenient time we can discuss the details.

Once you meet, share with them some details about the testimonial you envision. Tell them you don't want to them to lie, but you hope that your value has been obvious and helpful. Level with them too - tell them you are trying to create a *value* difference between you and all the other insurance agents in your market.

They will appreciate your honesty and if they value what you have done and are continuing to do for them, they will gladly say basically anything you suggest to them. I'm serious. Most people don't know what to say so you have to come prepared with a written testimonial that you would LOVE to share with others, and simply get their approval on it. I've had owners tell me to simply write it up and put their name on it with their phone number. No questions asked.

My primary goal, typically, is to get a video testimonial however. This will require you to coach the client as to what to say, in most cases. I use my Flip video camera and set it up on a mini tripod. There are two ways to do this:

1. Sit at a table and get an over-the-shoulder shot of the client sharing the testimonial with you.

2. Have the client stand in front of something at the business that others will recognize and record them sharing the testimonial.

Remember to tell your client that you would prefer they not talk about how much money you saved them, if in fact you saved them money. Ask them to talk about your value and how you have helped them solve a particular problem. If you got 20 of your best clients to do this for you and had all of these uploaded to a YouTube Channel, and on your website, how powerful would that be? Other people, in your community, would find these videos and be seriously impacted. It's a way to borrow trust from the tribe.

Value

What is *value* to your target client? This is the million dollar question. If you think what you are sharing with the prospect or client is *value* and they think it's crap, guess what, it's crap! Value is anything that helps your client produce or profit more.

I specialize in helping business owners, professionals and executives (a broad niche but I can do well within it because I have defined *value* accurately) – so I share marketing/sales and productivity strategies that will help them produce more.

This does not mean I share some *Wall Street Journal* link. Write your own articles; create your own videos; write your own thought-provoking quotes. Be an insurance artist.

Entertainment

Share *value* in a fun way. Show a video clip of you pulling a prank on the intern in your office. Keep it in good humor of course, but know that this is a great way to connect with your community who probably likes to laugh every now and then. It's not all about insurance. Remember, people could care less about insurance from a technical perspective. Incorporate some passion and creativity to get your message across at an emotional and fun level.

Education

Simply put – educate your community. Become a resource. The best insurance agent is not the one with a thousand initials after his or her name. It's the one who can clearly explain in simple terms what insurance means. Come up with fun "Did You Know" facts to share; like "Did you know that Business Income and Extra Expense coverage is an extra bucket of cash you can reach into while your business is down during a covered loss?"

Other examples include:

→ How-to videos and articles

→ Do-it-yourself videos (if you have contractors as clients, go on site and get them to talk you through a simple DIY while you record it with your Flip; give them props and link kickbacks in the credits; and share)

→ Articles on topics that HELP your community and establish you as a RESOURCE – the most important part of this is that you must WRITE YOUR OWN ARTICLES!

Conversation

Don't tell others how awesome you are. Please. It's annoying and no one cares. *"Did you know we have a combined 793 years of experience in our agency?"* That statement does nothing of value for your community. I can envision the person who is sharing this statement standing on their desk beating their chest like an ape.

Establish and foster a conversation by posing a question or thought that encourages dialogue amongst members. You can sit back like a proud parent and watch as community members begin dialoguing back and forth.

Listening

If someone is talking about you online and you don't hear it or read it, did it really happen? Yes it did.

Create for yourself a Google Alerts account to alert you of all key word searches performed on you (words you told Google Alerts were important to you to receive notification on – visit **www.google.com/alerts**).

Search Twitter for key words about you and your business. Search yourself online in Google. That's right, Google yourself. What comes up? If nothing, that doesn't make it a good thing. If someone says something bad about you and your business, RESPOND with the intent to LEARN what happened and HOW you can improve it moving forward.

And of course, publicly have the conversation online so that everyone can see that you are trying to take positive steps toward correcting a wrong. Solve the problem with the simplest and most direct solution. Learn from it.

Consistency

Be consistent. If you are going to post a quote each morning, you must be consistent about it. People learn to rely on systems and want to see you have established one built on valuable consistent content. Does consistent mean you have to post 15 pieces of content each day? I hope not – post during key times of day when your community is most likely to be listening.

Key times of day for optimum viewing tendencies are Tuesdays and Wednesdays between 10 a.m. and 3 p.m. (according to Mashable). We don't want to over inundate the community. Don't spam them. Be excellent, be without desire and be consistent. Be consistent with your value, listen to your community, respond with solutions and encourage meaningful conversations.

Authentic

Be transparent, be authentic, be YOU. Social media is a chatty medium, be authentic to your voice. The bottom line is to be clear with your content and who you are trying to help. The biggest secret of all is to be consistent and be YOU. It's about transparency. People want to know who you are and what you really think and feel.

7 KEY FACTORS FOR ENGAGEMENT

I have also developed 7 additional key factors to consider for optimum engagement with your community. These are things to consider when creating your social strategy.

1. **Where is your community online?**
   Where are your target clients online? Facebook is obviously hot right now. I follow St. Paul's advice in I Corinthians 9:22(b) – a stretch, I'll admit, for tying this to social media, but it works...

   22 ...I have become all things to all people so that by all possible means I might [save] some.

   What I mean here is simply this – if our prospects are on Facebook, that's where I'm going to be. If in three years they are all on some new network, that's where I'll be too.

In 2008, only 8% of Americans had Facebook accounts – according to a national survey in 2011, this has risen to 51%. Do we need more proof?

2. **When are they online?**
   Is your community comprised of late night owls? Watch the trends on your analytics to determine what content is being viewed at different hours of the day. You can begin to see trends when most of your community is online and listening.

3. **Social Factors**
   Economical, political and religious conditions; holidays, etc. Tailor your value message given the time of year. For instance, last Christmas, my ezine was going to be sent out on Christmas Eve. I knew that most people would be at home and not checking email but I still wrote a piece that related Miracle on 34th Street with business success. It received over one hundred click-thrus despite the holiday; it was a themed article and received positive feedback.

4. **Dinner or snack?**
Is your community in the mood for a 500 word blog post given the time of day, or would a thought provoking sentence be sufficient? A brief video clip (15-30 seconds) may work better during the day than at night. Consider what portion size your community prefers to digest given the time and day of week.

5. **Share info to get info.**
Urban Outfitters encouraged customers to send photos of their moms as part of a Mothers' Day contest; their own team members sent in photos too. This helped their community take interest and feel connected by submitting their own photos and participating. Would you be crossing the line by asking your community to upload a picture of their most recent claim? What if you uploaded one from yours? Just something to think about.

6. **It's not about the numbers.**
Your primary focus is defining value and creating the content. Once you have clearly defined value for your niche and community, consistently share it and they will come. *Field of Dreams* scenario. Just keep in mind, the buzz has worn off – people will click over you if they feel your message is the same thing, just refurbished. This raises the bar for personal excellence and creativity on your part. It's not how loud you shout, or even how much you are sharing; but rather, <u>what you are sharing</u>.

7. **ROI (Return on Investment)**
Soft Impact benefits would be things like branding; staying on top of the mind of your community; using it as a platform to showcase and become a resource for your community; create likeability and borrow trust to lead to next step (like sign-ups for your ezine, etc)

Hard impact benefits would be all about the dollars. Tracking links from Facebook and Twitter; and looking at customer interactions on your website. Google Analytics helps you determine how many people were driven to your site, and the particular links within it after any given post.

The primary goal is NOT sales – the primary goal is to build a culture of YOU and what you do. It's to increase word-of-mouth, likeability, trust and becoming a resource. This all leads to increased sales eventually, but what if it simply leads to more loyal customers?

Social media allows us to connect with others, create and gift our own version of art; and in the process, develop long-term profitable relationships. A well-developed and authentic social media strategy is a good supplement to a strong personal brand.

The young insurance professional of the future focuses her efforts on creating and gifting via social media as a means for attracting ideal clients and developing a value difference between herself and every other agent in her market. What kind of art are you going to create?

✖CHALLENGE | BECOME A CONSULTANT

Step 1 | Make a list of your top 5-10 clients (based on how well you get along with them, how little they bother you, how much commission you earn, how many referrals they have sent your way... basically, the clients you would clone if possible).

Step 2 | Analyze each client. What do they like? What are their hobbies? What is their age? Do they have children? Are they married? How long have they been married? Where do they live (neighborhood)? What kind of policies did you write for them? What made them buy from you?

If you are on Facebook with them, look over their profile and posts. Learn more about them and who they are. What is their business? What is their passion? What ideas can you offer that would help them get more of what they want? What kind of referrals would you need to find for them that would be of great value to them and their business?

Step 3 | Once you have answered these questions and have a good idea of WHO your client is, start developing a strategy. Consider yourself a consultant that offers ideas for helping people, just like your top 5% of clients, produce or profit more. What would you need to know more of? What books would you need to read? What articles? Who should you be connecting with?

When you start making friends with people your clients want to be friends with, you create an opportunity to connect others for their own good – this has a way of reciprocating itself in your favor.

PILLAR IV

"SELL"

IS FOR LEARNING HOW TO SELL WHEN "HOW TO SELL" IS OVER AND DEAD

10 | Why the Old Way of Selling Insurance Doesn't Work Anymore!

"Many a false step was made by standing still."

– Fortune Cookie

Insurance has been around since 2100 B.C. with The Code of Hammurabi. In *Chapter 1 | Prehistoric Thinking* we talked about spreading risk over a large group as a means for minimizing exposure to danger. The second notion of insurance is to *restore*. That's where Hammurabi comes in — his code (the law of the time) stated that a member of the community would have the loan on their dwelling forgiven if the dwelling was destroyed by <u>fire</u> or <u>flood</u>.

There were no Premiere Endorsements at that time. Fire. Flood. And people didn't argue with Hammurabi, he would kill you if you did. They considered it generous that the loan would be forgiven if one of the TWO natural disasters occurred. Only if you became disabled in some physical aspect that would prevent you from being able to pay off the loan, were you cut a break.

Today, many insureds feel that everything under the sun should be covered and there should be no consequence for turning in several claims in any given time period. Can you imagine if Hammurabi was your agent? You wouldn't even call him to turn in a claim unless your home was burnt to the ground!

Fortunately, the insurance industry has evolved over the years. In Medieval times, with the expansion of towns and trade, many guilds began to offer "insurance" protection to their members. They offered funeral expenses and support for immediate family of members who became very ill or died. The way it worked was simple; the older tradesman who owned the shop would hire on an apprentice and pay him *very little*. But, part of his keep was paid into the guild, which served as insurance for the perils mentioned above.

This was a huge incentive at that time and many farmers began to take up tradesman opportunities as a result. Over the hundreds of years that have since passed, although insurance (in my opinion) still improves your quality of living, it has become viewed as commodity. The insured has been conditioned to view insurance policies as the same product, the only difference being price. And today it is a marketed practice and belief!

The least liked profession in the world, next to attorneys and car salespeople, are insurance salespeople. This is because for decades upon decades our sales process was quite simple – it was all about The Law of Averages. This is the mindset of "throwing as much mud against the wall because eventually something will stick." That sales approach is the reason you, as a young insurance professional, feel as though you are being held at arm's length constantly when trying to engage a prospect.

When I joined the industry in 2009 I did exactly what I saw every other agent doing – I quoted. I would give anyone a quote, no hassles, no obligations; you got your doggone quote from me. I hate *that* word now. I don't use it. I refuse to use the term "quote." Even in conversation with someone who is not talking to me about buying insurance, if they use the word "quote," I will rephrase when I respond by saying "proposal." A word like "quote" implies commodity.

You may have noticed that prospects will set the rules of the game or establish their own verbal contract with you up front. "I would like a quote on auto insurance, just give me an apples to apples comparison. I want to see if you can save me some money on my premiums." And you nod your head and ask them for their data, like date of birth, social security number (and you're quick to inform them that you need their social security number because of something called "insurance scoring" where their credit rating is taken into account with their premium – way to go ace). You go back to your ivory tower and enter in all of the data and begin praying to the insurance gods that you can rip their price down low enough that they will switch over to you. That's the wrong game plan.

That's why you see so many bitter old agents in this industry who have a very thick skin and sarcastic vibe to them. When you permit yourself to be treated like commodity over and over again it chips away at your moral fiber. You begin to reflect someone who feels cheated. You hold a disdain for others. You begin to hate what you do. You don't own your business, you own a job.

I wasn't always an insurance agent. I used to be the insured, and I know what it felt like to be around a cliché insurance agent. I had this built-in sales radar that blinked louder when I was around one. I remember when I talked with any type of salesperson I would immediately put up my guard because I had this perception of salespeople as though they were trained killers. They were going to try to talk me into buying something I didn't want. They knew the tricks and how to manipulate words. So before a salesperson would even talk to me I would have this built-in disdain for them. They haven't even said a word to me yet and I would shut down.

Think about your prospects. Do you think they are excited to meet with you? Most likely not. They have been conditioned over decades to resist you, thanks in part to our forefathers approach to selling insurance and the taboo of insurance salespeople in general. But do they tell you they hate you? Of course not. They establish their rules and you must abide by them. Start quoting.

I remember quoting up policies for prospects and presenting to them all of my hard work and they would respond, "This looks really good, let me think on this for a couple days and I'll call you back." I would be ecstatic, "Oh man! I got a sale baby!" I would get in my salvage titled Honda Civic and be fist pumping at how excited I was. Do you think the prospect called me back in a couple days like he said he would? No. What did I do? I called him back. I left messages. I became the prover-bial *emotionally attached ex-girlfriend* who just couldn't let it go. Eventually he would answer his phone and tell me, "Well, my old agent was able to come back at a lower price so I'm just going to stay where I'm at. Thanks for all your hard work though." Devastating.

It was during this difficult time of selling that I began studying great sales minds like Jeffrey Gitomer, David Sandler, Zig Ziglar, Ed Lamont, and Jeff Wodicka. I began to understand that the reason prospects treat insurance salespeople the way they do is because we have conditioned them to do so. We are the reason prospects push back and put up walls around themselves. They are trying to protect themselves because they have either had a bad experience with a salesperson once, or the connotation of insurance sales conjures up images of polyester suits and slicked back hair.

I also began to learn that systems of sales don't work anymore. Don't buy books on "how to close" because nobody wants to be closed. Do you want to be closed by someone? Of course not. If a prospect likes you, believes in you and your product, and trusts you, then they will most likely buy from you. But the process of selling insurance requires you to think and act differently than all of that garbage the forefathers of traditional insurance selling taught you. Systems of sales and closes are out. So where do you begin?

11 | How to Prospect Like a Member of the Top 10%

"You cannot fail at prospecting unless

you fail to prospect."

-- David Sandler,
Founder of the Sandler Sales Institute
and Sandler Selling System

Two of the most common questions all new producers ask are, *"Where* do I get new business leads?" and *"How* do I find new prospects?" I know this because I asked the exact same questions when I first joined the industry as a fully licensed producer. But before you can even begin to ask that question you need to know *who* it is you want to be doing business with.

If you focus on personal lines then you will prospect differently than if you are strictly a commercial lines producer. I write from the perspective of a commercial producer who also has the capability to write personal. I don't go out looking for auto, homeowners and personal umbrella policies. I attract those. I do actively pursue commercial prospects. The good news is that several of the prospecting strategies I am going to outline for you in this chapter can be used for both lines! Let's start at the beginning of any prospecting strategy though...

WHAT'S YOUR NICHE?

"Find a niche, not a nation."
— Seth Godin

When determining your niches ask yourself what you like. What are your hobbies? What are you passionate about? Do you like working on cars? Modifying them? Or, do you like working out? 5ker? If yes to both, then your niches for the first quarter are body shops, gyms, and anyplace where you will find individuals of like mind and interest. Each quarter I choose 1-2 niches based on my interests and begin to develop my *suspect* list.

If I hate working around the house, and my wife is better at fixing plumbing issues than me, why in the *world* would I make my niche "plumbing contractors"? That's ridiculous. Make a list of everything you like and know something about. Those are your niches.

Once you have determined your niches, think about how you can break these down further...

Let's look at Matt and Brian. Both have been in the insurance industry for two years and are fully licensed. Both are compiling a suspect list they hope to scrub into awesome prospects. Matt's list is titled "Restaurants." It includes all restaurants in a 30 mile radius.

Brian, on the other hand, has a suspect list titled "Fine Dining Restaurants with Less than 30% alcohol sales and a Chamber endorsement." Brian's list is going to be a lot smaller than Matt's. But guess what? If he familiarizes himself with this specific niche and their needs, he will be working smarter by becoming a specialist in this niche.

> "Suspects" are one step behind "prospects". Suspects are names of businesses or individuals who have made your initial list but must undergo further examination before making your Prospect List. Suspects could be too small, too large, maybe they wouldn't meet your underwriting criteria, maybe you find out they are someone you don't want to do business with.

A smaller niche list of prospects is not a problem assuming you familiarize yourself with the product (insurance policies/coverages) and are able show the decision-maker the value in doing business with you. I'm not here to teach you the products in your agency, but I can help you understand how to work significantly smarter than your competition and how to create a value-difference in the eyes of your potential insured.

IDENTIFYING IDEAL PROSPECTS

There are several ways to effectively identify who you could potentially take to market just by looking at the surface and getting some background information. These background efforts on your part can save you drastic amounts of time (which is money) spent creating mailings and cold-calling in person on businesses who may not fit your mold anyways.

Let's look at a few ways you can pre-qualify who is your ideal prospect – someone you are going to actually reach out to and engage about their insurance protection plan.

The top 7 resources I use every time for scrubbing my list online are below:

→ Google

→ YouTube

→ Facebook Pages (for businesses)

→ Twitter

→ Linkedin

→ Reference USA online directory

→ Google Earth

I use all of these resources for both personal and commercial lines prospecting. The objective is to determine if this is someone (or a business) that you are going to be able to underwrite. Is this someone you will want to do business with? Maybe the account is too small after you look into it more. Maybe the account is too big! Do you think you'll find a decision maker for Starbucks in your local market? Nope. The free world-class tools that the internet provides you for qualifying suspects into prospects saves you hours of effort.

For example, if you are searching a particular restaurant and find they have a Facebook Page, but soon notice they are posting pictures of patrons passed out at tables from the night before while partying... you may have an underwriting issue. Wouldn't it be helpful to know this BEFORE you go to the trouble of spending money on a mailing, the mileage for the appointment, the time wasted to get prepared for the meeting, etc?

You could use Linkedin to search suspects/prospects by name and determine who your mutual connections are – could this third-party connect both of you and give you a recommendation?

Reference USA is a great tool to use to determine what kind of insurance budget businesses have. These kinds of figures are available in their online database. I obtained mine by opening an account at the Columbus Metropolitan Library. Once you have your library card you receive free access to Reference USA online through their website.

Reference USA has many library clients who have done this for connecting with their business clients by offering this resource for free. Take full advantage of this, and thank you to Chris Neeson and Amy Greene at Ohio Mutual Insurance Group for sharing this tip with me when I first started in the business!

Finally, if you think your underwriters aren't already searching businesses on these networks too, think again. If you see something funky on a Facebook Page, keep in mind that if you just 'slide' it on through to your underwriter like "I didn't see anything strange..." you are going to begin chipping away at your own credibility. Scrub the list, scrub it good.

GETTING THE PROSPECT'S ATTENTION

Once you know who your ideal prospects are, how do you get in front of them? How do you get their attention? How do you begin to develop these quality leads? Those were the questions I had when I first started. Once you know your niches and who your ideal prospects are, you must identify the most effective approaches and strategies for connecting with them.

Keep in mind, I don't advocate traditional techniques because they don't work as effectively as more uncommon strategies I have found to be effective. But for the sake of giving you options, I have listed several ways you can get in front of your niche/ideal prospect, see below:

→ Cold call, the **traditional** "dialing for dollars" approach

→ **Traditional** door to door cold calling

→ Chamber of Commerce networking events

→ Cross-sell commercial clients on personal lines products

→ Referral/Lead generating organizations like BNI

→ Get involved in local organizations like Rotary, Lions Club, Optimists, Kiwanis, etc

→ Volunteer at your church or in local youth sports programs

→ Buy leads

→ Leverage social media/social networking

→ Participate in trade shows

→ Join associations of the niches you are focused on helping

→ Speak to groups of prospects at any organization, club, or association that will listen

→ Write advertorials (an article you write in a magazine that your prospects will read)

→ And so on...

These are all valid ways to get a prospect's attention, but they are not all good. Traditional methods for selling insurance like cold calling or door to door selling are better known as "interruptions." Do you want to be known as an interruption? I don't.

You want to become known as a person of value and you want to touch as many people as you can with your value message. After six months of traditional insurance selling (which was horrible by the way) I began to notice that the people who spoke at chamber events would typically have 3 to 5 individuals come up and speak to them afterwards.

If the person speaking was even mildly humorous and offered some decent insight about something of value to the audience, there could be as many as 10 or more people crowding around them after they left the stage or podium. I thought to myself, "This is a lot easier way to prospect." So I began to speak about things that my audience would find of value, which was *not* insurance. I spoke about marketing and social media strategies for business because my target prospects were business owners, professionals and executives.

This is valuable information for my ideal prospects, and I wanted them to really listen to me and start to like me. If they liked me and my message then they would want to talk to me after the event. Which they did. I got smarter after a couple events and would have a sign-up form on each table for those listening to sign-up for my weekly ezine that would have a marketing tip for them. No insurance lingo. No gimmicks. And sign-up they did!

I racked up nearly 500 emails in about eighteen months of speaking locally in the communities I wanted to do business in. What do you think happens when someone gets an email each week at the same time that causes them to stop and think in terms of Matt Brown, appreciate the value nugget of info I *gift* to them, and who also – oh by the way – is an insurance agent? That's right. I would receive emails back from subscribers who were interested in talking about their auto, homeowners, life or business insurance, and so on.

But let's focus on the fundamentals, even traditional forms of prospecting are gold mines assuming you know how to do them *right*.

THE ULTIMATE NON-CLICHÉ SALES LETTER THAT WORKS!

"They say I'm old-fashioned, and live in the past,
but sometimes I think progress progresses too fast!"
— Dr. Seuss

I write sales letters and mail them to my commercial prospects. But I don't write sales letters like all the other insurance agents and direct writers do. I don't claim to be able to save people 40% off their insurance premiums. I don't tell the reader they should call me for a no-hassle, no obligation free quote. I also don't write two pages of size 11 font, single-spaced, sales jargon, that is mailed in a very obvious insurance company or agency envelope. Why? Because I have watched my wife (at home) and Principal (at Hays Insurance Agencies, where I serve as a Producer) both sift through incoming mail.

My wife stands over the kitchen trash can and sorts through all mail and anything that looks even questionably like spam gets trashed. Then she opens the other letters and gives them about a 10 second look over. If that letter doesn't grab her attention in that time span she rips it in half and trashes it.

The Principal at our agencies gets tons of sales literature, but guess what? He has a line of defense – the CSR. Our CSR gets the mail each day at the post office and then goes through each piece, making an executive decision on which should get put in his "A" pile, "Magazine" pile, and "trash pile"... which goes immediately into the trash. I have watched countless sales letters get trashed before they were even opened because the salesperson mailed it in a lame envelope that reeked of "sales letter."

So I determined to do **two** things:

1. Create an envelope that will make the cut to "A" pile for a business owner and get a chance to be read, as well as...

2. Write a letter that compels the reader to stop and think for a moment about me and how I could potentially help them.

My sales letters do not ask the prospect to call me. They are just "pre-cold call warm-up letters." As far as the envelope approaches I have found most effective, there are two so far.

I have used a plain white envelope, with the <u>hand-written</u> name of the business owner and mailing address to the business location, and no return mail address of my agency at all. I do this because I have noticed that my wife will open any hand-written addressed envelope that does not have a return address on it. It gets a chance to be read. That's all that matters to me.

The second route is to use the largest manila envelope you can find, I'm talking 9"x12". Take a Sharpie and do the same thing you did with the plain white envelope, hand write the name of the owner and their mailing address. I don't recommend you write your agency name and address on the return address section. I would just put your PO Box, city, state and zip.

Writing your return address can screw you up more often than not. If you put the agency and address, the owner may have a gate-keeper who will recognize this as potential spam and trash it.

For a while, instead of writing our agency PO Box address on the return address, I would instead use my name [M. Brown] and put "Suite 295" (instead of PO Box 295) and then city, state and zip. Of course I had a piece of mail sent back for whatever reason and the post office called our agency and told me they didn't want me putting "Suite 295" on future mailings, "Just use PO Box like everyone else, Matt." I used "Suite" so it would appear more professional... and the point was to <u>not</u> be like everyone else. Oh well.

I'm not saying I don't trust our postal service, I have a great respect for what they do, however, there have been times when an owner has told me he or she never received my letter. You may opt to mail it first class, depending on how many you are mailing.

Another **tip**, use <u>stamps</u> on your mailings. Don't have the post office print the postage on the envelopes – this is a huge giveaway for "bulk mailing". (This also means the likelihood of your envelope making the desk of the prospect is LESS LIKELY).

What does your sales letter look like Matt? I know you want to ask that. Here is one example of a sales letter I have used:

> *Dear Mr. Jones,*
>
> *My name is Matt Brown.*
>
> *I'm a **restaurant insurance doctor** (I know what it sounds like) BUT I'm <u>not</u> asking for a handout or a chance to quote your policies.*
>
> ***What I am offering****...*
>
> *A **20 minute conversation** with you about your restaurant property and liability protection plan, to determine <u>if</u> I would be able to help you solve any problems.*
>
> *After we talk, if I feel that I can help, I'll tell you so. If I don't think I can at this time, I'll tell you that too. I value your time and my own.*
>
> *I will call the restaurant in the next week to determine when the best time would be for us to meet and chat.*
>
> *Very truly yours (and I **really** mean that),*
>
> *Matt Brown*
> *The Insurance Producer*

Now, as you can see on my template, my sales letter is brief and to the point. But I bet you are thinking, "What kind of brochure do you put in with your letter?" I have discovered that people don't really care about you or your agency.

They don't care that you've been in business for 168 years. They don't care that your last name is the same name as the agency. They don't care that you have a *really* special program that can help their business.

Remember what we talked about in the first half of the book? Create a <u>value difference</u> between you and every other agent they've received sales materials from.

Here's what I suggest you include with your sales letter:

→ An article (copied out of local newspaper) of you and regarding some kind of business accomplishment that you have been recognized for.

→ An article YOU wrote that got published in print media (magazine or newspaper, etc.) that would make a good business impression on the prospect.

→ An idea (or several) that would specifically help their business produce or profit more. Sounds like our definition of "value"... strange.

Doesn't matter if you have a *fancy shmancy* folder with your agency logo and picture on it. That's a waste of money on your agency's part if there is no value to put in to share with your prospect. The challenge is yours – get in your local print media for business success. Copy the article. Put it in with your sales letter. That's *value*. They will stop and think about you in a positive light.

EXPECT OBJECTIONS AND ASK THE RIGHT QUESTIONS

Before following up on your sales letter you must understand what **Objections** are and what **Questions** you should be asking in any given conversation with a prospect.

Identifying Common Objections

Objections are really just questions in statement format. They initially frustrate us because we don't like friction. But friction is good because it helps us solve problems and connect with the prospect.

Here is a list of the 15 most common objections I have encountered:

1. I only deal locally.
2. That's too high of a price.
3. I don't like that company.
4. My agent is a good friend of mine.
5. I actually have a claim open right now.
6. I'll need to speak to the other partners about this.
7. I just renewed.
8. I've not heard of your agency.
9. I don't need an umbrella policy.
10. I don't need EPLI.
11. I don't need higher limits of liability.
12. I don't need life insurance.
13. I'd like to think about it.
14. I'm going to shop around and get back to you.
15. I've been with ABC Agency for thirty years.

Objections arise because the prospect perceives no value, no trust, or they feel they don't have a need for a particular coverage you are offering. You need to be asking the right questions and hopefully have conveyed your value in the steps leading up to these objections.

There are many ways to work through objections and I don't believe that a sales book can teach you how to as effectively as in a workshop setting, and by role-playing with others. If you are looking for a blue-print guide with exactly what to say in response to every objection listed, this is not the book.

Asking The Right Questions

> *"Successful people ask better questions, and as a result,*
> *they get better answers."*
> — Tony Robbins, American Self-Help Author and Life Success Coach

Questions steer people. They don't manipulate situations, they refine them. They help us discover what is really at the core. Top producers speak only 20-30% of the time in conversation with a prospect. Question and listen.

If you spend your time at an appointment preaching about how awesome you and your company are, you will have annoyed another prospect and lost out on an opportunity to develop a long-term relationship. Questioning is truly the best technique for uncovering, learning and connecting with a prospect.

However, the wrong question can kill a first impression <u>and</u> your chances of engaging a prospect, so before we even begin talking with a prospect I feel it would be fitting to share what <u>NOT</u> to ask!

In Ed Lamont's brilliant guide entitled *Street Smart Selling*, he shares several **Trust-Destroying Questions**. (I strongly urge you to invest in Ed's guide at www.lamontconsultinggroup.com/products, do it now.)

→ ...how about I stop by and try to save you a little money?

→ ...how much did you pay for insurance last year?

→ ...can I bring my quote in last?

→ ...you're not going to show my quote to anyone else, are you?

→ ...do you want me to go back and ask for a better price?

It would make sense to most of us that the above questions are the sign of your typical cliché insurance salesperson that no one wants to listen to. Don't be *that guy (*or *girl)*.

Proper questioning keeps you in control of the conversation. If you ever feel a conversation is getting away from the topic you want it to be on, simply use an open-ended question to get back on topic. Open-ended questions begin with *what*, *how* or *why*.

Sample Open-Ended Questions:

→ Price aside, what is most important to you about your protection plan?

→ Why did you go with that particular agency?

→ What did the referral say about them?

→ What would you change about your current insurance experience if price was not an obstacle?

→ What are your expectations of your insurance agent?

FOLLOWING UP ON YOUR ULTIMATE SALES LETTER

Following up on your sales letter can be done in one of two ways. In person OR phone call. Gauge this on the proximity of the prospects that made your list. If they are all in one town then you could visit them all in person (you can batch them together like this on one particular day of the week).

But also keep in mind that this is still technically a "cold call," even though you have warmed it up with a letter and some print media value or an idea that is going to help them. I still don't want to be viewed as an interruption.

Do you value your time? The business owner and/or decision maker you want to talk with values their time too. Also, how do you know they are going to be at the business at the time you arrive? If you drive 20 minutes and find out they don't come into the shop on Tuesdays, then that was a waste of a drive and time.

I typically follow up on my letters with a <u>phone call</u> and there are three reasons I do this:

1. Supposing they have received my letter and read it, along with the value clipping included, they <u>should</u> have a pretty good idea of who I am and why I am calling.

2. I will get the gatekeeper first, in most cases. I love the gatekeeper. If you can build rapport with them and strike a brief friendship, you can get access to valuable information... like the best time of day to get in touch with the decision maker, etc.

3. If I get the decision maker on the first call, I can perform an initial *analysis* and gauge if there are any pains or problems that would give me a reason to come and visit in person so we can determine how I can help.

I have included one of the most common conversations that take place when I call my prospect(s). This scenario includes a common objection <u>and</u> how I dig beneath the surface of that objection to find out if there are any issues that could warrant an appointment with me.

You must test and overcome cliché *safe phrases* and responses that you receive from decision makers in order to determine if they are just trying to brush you off. Remember, they are used to the old school way of selling and are just waiting for you to drop a line or a close they've heard before... the good news is you don't use cliché sales lines or closes. Your job is to help them solve problems and sometimes you have to dig beneath the surface to help them identify a problem or pain. Sounds like something a doctor would do...

In this example, the prospect and I are talking on the phone together – pretend with me that we are already past the gatekeeper.

Me: "Mr. Jones, my name is Matt Brown and I mailed you a very large manila envelope last week regarding your restaurant's property and liability insurance. Do you have a moment to discuss that with me?"

I always ask a prospect if they *have a moment* to discuss their insurance plan with me because I respect their time.

Prospect: "I do remember getting that in the mail, but I've got tell you, I've been with ABC Agency for thirty years."

This is one of the most common objections I hear and most times it's just a safe phrase a prospect uses to defend themselves from someone like you.

Me: "Oh I see, are you concerned our meeting would be a waste of time then?"

Maybe they feel that taking the time to meet with me would be a waste of time, so I put it out there on the table.

Prospect: "Well, kind of."

Me: "Why so?"

I'm digging deeper. I need to know what it is *specifically* about this prospect's current insurance experience that is giving him a reason to say he doesn't want to talk with me.

Prospect: "Well, I go to the same church as the agent and know his family really well."

Me: "Oh I see, so you're worried that if me and you were to work together it would ruin a good friendship you have with your current agent?"

Prospect: "Yes."

OK, so I understand why he initially thought our meeting would be a waste of time. It had nothing to do with ABC Agency; instead, he is friends with the agent. I can appreciate that, but sometimes agents take their friends' business lightly and for granted. It happens all the time. Press in a little deeper...

Me: "I know ABC Agency, they do a great job of taking care of their clients. Who is your agent?"

Prospect: "Jim Smith."

Me: "I don't know Jim personally, but I'm sure he does an excellent job for you. I'm not trying to take away that relationship you have with him. But when was the last time you and Jim reviewed your policies together?"

Prospect: "Umm... it's been a few years."

Me: "Would you say it's been more than three years since you reviewed them together?"

Prospect: "Yes, probably closer to four."

Me: "Hmm. Well I don't want to waste your time Mr. Jones, or my own, but what would you say to me and you reviewing your policies together? If we don't find any problems or gaps that would be important to your business then I'll tell you so and we can part as friends. Does that sound fair to you?"

I want the prospect to stop and think about how Jim Smith, his agent, has been serving him and his best interests over the years. When I say, "Hmm" it's because I feel that a good agent reviews policies with clients each year. Things change and so do the needs of the client. He could be paying for something he doesn't need, or have a gap in coverage that could put him in a world of hurt if not resolved.

There is no "hard close" at the end, only me asking the prospect if he thinks it would be fair for us to meet and review his policies together. At this point he may be thinking that Jim could be doing a little better job in the department of servicing his account, so he may agree to meeting with me.

Your entire objective on the initial phone sales call is to get an appointment. At the appointment you can prove your value and try to identify problems.

12 | The Appointment: 5 Key Points You Must Cover With Your Prospect!

"Restore a man to his health, his purse lies

open to thee."

– Robert Burton

I believe that if you want to belong to the top 10% of young insurance professionals in this industry then you are going to have to separate your selling style and philosophy from the other 90% of your competitors. This is not hard to do because at least 90% of insurance professionals sell insurance using The Law of Averages (quoting and hoping).

The difficult part is committing to this new way of selling. So once you have an appointment with an ideal prospect, how do you determine if this is someone you are going to take to market and what is the structure to the appointment?

This is a book, not a workshop. Remember, when in conversation with people there is no script. There is no system of selling. There is a process and key indications that will prompt you to respond a particular way; or you may need to probe in a little deeper with a specific question to get to the bottom of what the prospect is saying; but there is no script.

After my sales letter has been sent and I have been able to confirm an appointment with the prospect, it's time to start thinking like a doctor getting ready to see a patient. I am going to relate much of my selling process to that of a doctor because of my background at the hospitals and my interaction with medical professionals.

Through my own trials and errors over the past few years, I have found that there are *5 Key Points* that must be covered in each appointment before you can resolve to take this prospect to market. In order for you to do any work on a policy, your prospect and you will need to move through each key point and make sure you are both on the same page. There's no manipulating in this sales process.

To simplify *The Insurance Xperience Sales Philosophy* it would be, "Make friends, set fair rules, identify problems, talk about their budget and make sure you are dealing with the decision maker." It's a genuine approach to selling insurance and helping someone solve problems. Many times in insurance, however, the prospect doesn't know they have a problem. Your job is to be a professional and bring a problem to light and help provide a solution ONLY if, and when, the prospect is in agreement.

If you are trying to have an intellectual debate with your prospect as to why they need Business Income coverage, you will lose. You have to speak to the prospect in emotional terms and bring out how this problem could potentially put them in a world of hurt if they don't invest in it. No insurance professional is up-selling a prospect by trying to ensure they are well protected for the potential losses and exposures they face in their given business. *Unless you present it as an up-sell.*

I'm going to go into depth on each of the **5 Key Points** that you need to establish in your appointment, sometimes you won't make it through all five points in the first appointment, and it depends on how the conversation goes. After describing each of the key points I will share some examples of appointments I've been on and what common objections are typically raised and how you can respond. I will also share common pitfalls and mistakes that are made and how you can avoid them and help your prospect hedge against a potential loss that they didn't think about before meeting with you. Let's begin!

#1 MAKE FRIENDS

When I'm given the opportunity to meet with a new prospect, my goal is to make friends with them. I want to develop long-lasting friendly business relationships with my clients. The appointment is an opportunity to set a great first impression and begin a new friendship. What's the first thing you do when you meet the new prospect? Smile, make eye-contact and shake their hand firmly. Do you remember firm handshakes? No. Do you remember limp-wristed handshakes? Yes. Don't give them a limp-wristed handshake.

This is commonly referred to as building *rapport*, which means "to bring together" or "share a common goal." Find the middle ground where you both click. What do you do that *they* do? What do you like that *they* like?

- → Did you go to the same college as the decision maker?
- → Do you have any mutual connections or friends that the social networks showed?
- → Have they received any recent awards or recognitions?
- → Have they been published in any print media recently?

Look around and find common connectors:

- → Do you both have kids? Are they the same age?
- → Trophies and awards?
- → Books?
- → Pictures of recognizable people and them together?

You are trying to find at least one area where you can talk and connect with the decision maker. Do you both golf? Get them talking about *them* and find a way to connect during the conversation. This is where some sales training systems talk about "Type" selling.

There are hundreds of thousands of books that focus on type selling. I believe there is a psychology behind selling; but I'm not subscribing to the mindset that I need to know how to read a prospect's eyes and body movements in order to gauge where we stand during the sales meeting. This is all about manipulation and it makes me feel icky. I don't do it and I don't recommend it.

People like people who are similar to them. They like people who behave similar to them. We all do. It makes you feel more comfortable with the other person when you have commonalities. Your objective is to find the commonalities and harmonize. That would also mean don't blatantly mirror everything they are doing either, that's lame and feels manipulative. Harmonize your voice and body language with that of the prospect.

I remember listening to a David Sandler seminar on CD and he asked, "What do you say when the prospect offers you a cup of coffee?" One participant said, "Say 'yes please'," and Sandler replied, "No, you ask the prospect, 'Are you having a cup, sir?'"

The point is that this prospect may hate coffee but is just being polite, if you say "yes" because you think it makes him or her feel better about having their offer accepted, you could be wrong. You could ruin the entire appointment because now the prospect has to go get you a cup of Joe. Never assume. Harmonize and focus on laying the ground for a healthy, long-term relationship.

#2 ESTABLISH RULES OF THE GAME

If you must play, decide on three things at the start:
the rules of the game, the stakes, and the quitting time.
— Chinese Proverb

New producers are typically so excited at the opportunity to meet with a new prospect that they don't establish the rules of the game upfront. When you don't establish what your expectations are, as well as those of the prospect, and make sure they align – you are wasting yours, your agency and your prospect's time.

Most agents and producers go into an appointment, obtain the data needed to give a quote, and go back to their ivory tower and do their work hoping that they can rip the price down based on an apple to apple comparison. Bad game plan.

After a few minutes of connecting on a topic of mutual interest and warming up to each other it's time to give the appointment its direction. This is the part you most likely skip over currently and let the prospect state the reason for your being there. More often than not, a prospect will tell you, "Here's why I agreed to see you today... let's see if you can save me some money on my insurance premiums..."

This is not why you wanted to see them and you should have given them some sort of indication of why you wanted to meet with them on your initial phone call (refer back a few pages). This is the key point where you separate yourself from all other insurance salespeople your prospect has ever met.

Here's what I normally start by saying, "Mr. Jones, before we dig in here, I want to let you know that I'm probably not going to be able to save you any money on your insurance premiums. I won't be able to do an apples to apples comparison either. What I do is try to determine what problems you are having with your current insurance program and what solutions I can provide. If we can't find some problems together that need to be solved then I can save you and me a lot of time by telling you I can't help you at this time. Does that sound fair to you?"

Does it always sound like that? No, this isn't a script. The main points you want to make clear are (1) you're probably not going to be the cheapest option or save them any money, (2) and you only do work if there are problems to be solved. Take your profession seriously. Consider yourself a doctor, a *risk* doctor. You meet with a patient and diagnose pains. If you find no pains to provide a remedy for, then why would you write a prescription? That would be unprofessional.

This provides a fork in the road and you will get either a "yes" or "no" response. If you get a "Yes, that seems fair," then you can move on to asking some key questions to get the prospect talking about their current insurance experience and any changes they would make to it.

"No" responses to your up front contract or rules for the meeting require you to listen and understand the objection, because that's what it will be – an objection to your rules. Price objections right off the bat are a concern. I don't want to be fighting on price the entire appointment, that's why I lay it out early in the appointment that I probably won't be the cheapest option.

If their response to your verbal "contract" is, "Well, my prices have been going up year after year so I don't want to be paying more for insurance," then all you reply with is, "If we can't find some issues that need to be resolved in this meeting then don't worry,

I'm not going to waste your time." Price is almost always the first concern. Deal with it and stand firm that you probably won't save them any money.

You will be the first insurance professional to approach them and be completely honest with them in regards to saving money. Most insurance salespeople use potential premium savings as a way to get a shot at giving them a quote. Hours and dignity wasted.

Getting past this second Key Point is hard for most young agents because you really want their business. You may not have anything in the pipeline this month and the opportunity to work on their account is so exciting that you begin to think to yourself, "Well, you never know, they may be with a company that I know I can crush their price!"

Just because they brought up price doesn't mean it's the only concern. Without digging in and asking questions to diagnose the situation, you may never learn that their current billing plan is really hurting them because payments fall due during a time of year when cash flow is not readily available, like it is at other times of the year. Maybe they asked their agent to help solve this problem and he never got back to them. You never know!

3 Things I Would Never agree to while discussing our *rules of the game*:

1 | There will be multiple agents offering proposals

> I need to know if there are other agents bidding, especially if this is at renewal time. If there are others presenting I want to know who they are. If there is more than one other agent bidding, then I'm probably not going to offer a proposal UNLESS I know who the other agents are and I feel I have competitive markets and have established a *value difference* throughout our initial meeting. I've got to feel good about it by the end of the meeting or else I'm walking.

> If I know that price is the only thing that matters and the other markets being represented are more competitive than mine for this particular business then I'm

not going to stick around to be told "no." In fact, I make it a point to tell the prospect that I'm not going to be the lowest priced proposal. I will ask them what their decision is going to be based on, "Is price the only factor in your decision making process?" If "Yes," start walking.

2 | Apples to apples quote

No, I won't do it. I can't stand it when prospects ask me to work up an *apples to apples* so they can compare the price. How do they know that what they have is adequate? And why in the *world* are you just duplicating someone else's work? This is why it is critical that you identify problems or pains in your appointment at the beginning, immediately after building rapport and agreeing upon the rules of the game. If you don't begin by questioning and uncovering problems, then all you can do is take down their data and become an order-taker. Be a professional and focus on helping them solve problems, not duplicating a policy that may in fact be really great coverage.

3 | Dealing with a non-decision maker

When you get into larger commercial accounts, many times you will have a representative of the owner who meets with you and gives you the data you need. But I don't do data only. I need to know what's important. Sure, I'll talk with the non-decision making representative, but if I feel they are just going to take the proposal and drop it on the owner's desk to review with no recommendation and no passion for the problems I solved, then I'm not wasting my time.

In the end, the young insurance professional who establishes the rules of the game up front will improve their closing ratios dramatically; decrease the amount of time you waste quoting and chasing accounts who were never going to switch to you anyways; and take pride in knowing you are one of FEW who take the time do so.

#3 DIAGNOSE PAINS AND PROBLEMS

My current family doctor was the doctor who delivered me... at my birth. He has been a part of our family's medical history since my dad was a young man. I have learned a lot from this man. He is engaging, a good listener, and helps make sense of pains. Questioning and listening. Questioning and listening. That is his method for getting to the root of any situation. He asks questions and will probe with particular phrases that allow his patients to think and clarify their pains or concerns.

We don't know we have a problem, physically speaking, until the doctor runs some tests and asks us questions that bring the pains to light. Doctors get you talking about your pains and once clearly identified, they offer a solution to remedy or cure that pain. That's the approach I use in my appointments with prospects. They are my patient at that moment. I am interviewing them and trying to determine what kind of pain they are experiencing.

CREATING YOUR INSURANCE XPERIENCE ANALYSIS PACKET

So you are sitting across from the prospect and getting ready to identify some problems and pains. In the past, this is when you would probably take out your ACORD forms and start gathering data. That's lame. Or maybe you used a yellow legal pad? That's even worse. How comfortable are your underwriters with you taking this stuff out on an appointment to gather information?

I created my own Insurance Xperience Analysis packet. Some call it a Survey Kit. Tailor it to be all about the prospect and their business. You should have a picture of their business or logo on the front of the Packet, along with their business name. You can see an example of what I use on the following pages - do you notice it doesn't have any room for your name or your agency's? That's because no one cares, remember?

I create a *value difference* and positive impression with my prospect right off the bat with my Insurance Xperience Analysis packet, and you can too! I did all of this on Microsoft Word, it's very simple to do.

Title Page:

All about the prospect. Doesn't look like your boring ACORD forms, does it?

INSURANCE XPERIENCE ANALYSIS

PICTURE OF PROSPECT'S
BUSINESS OR THE
PROSPECT'S LOGO

NAME OF BUSINESS
NAME OF DECISION MAKER

Page 2: Service Expectations

I want to find out more about the business, the prospect, and what their pains and problems are. Uncover problems. Prioritize them.

SERVICE EXPECTATIONS

Questions To Prospect

What would you fix about your current insurance experience?

☐ Accessibility to Agent
☐ Billing
☐ How policy changes are handled
☐ Etc

Who is your current agency? Agent? Company? Have you ever had any issues with _____ that weren't handled the way you wanted?

What does perfect service mean to you? Are you getting this kind of service right now?

How often does your agent get out to see you? Is it important to you to see your agent _____ times per year to review coverage and overall operations?

Priority	Problem
1	
2	
3	
4	
5	

Page 3: Protection Review

Review their protection plan with them. Don't offer solutions at this time. Your job at this moment is to identify problems with their protection plan, which varies from business to business. If they don't agree it's important to them, then it doesn't make the list. Likewise, if you don't find any coverage problems, be a professional and tell them they're well-taken care of.

Page 4: Data Analysis

Much of this page includes details like the prospect's business and individual name, date of birth, social security number, tax ID number, address, and other common data. You should have much of this filled in already – which will make you appear knowledgeable and proactive. To be honest, much time is not spent on this page, just make sure you have the data you need like gross sales receipts, or payroll, depending on the risk.

Name of Insured(s) Business Name

Mailing Address
Cell   Email   Office/Home

Corporation   Individual   Joint Venture   LLC   Partnership
Trust (if applicable)

Years in Business   Total Annual Sales   SS#   Date of Birth   Tax ID#

Premises Information

Local	Bldg#	Street; City, County, Zip	City Limits (In/Out)	Interest (Owner/Tenant)	YR Built	#Emp.	Annual Sales	% Occupied

Tour of Property .... ☐ YES .... ☐ NO
Video .... ☐ YES .... ☐ NO
Pictures .... ☐ YES .... ☐ NO

Important Information To Remember To Ask:

Page 5: Notes Page

I don't take the yellow legal pad because I know you *do*.

N O T E S

Page 6: Budget and Decision Maker

I have found that if it's on paper and in bold print, it means you need it or you can't move forward. When you get to your budget step and identifying any final decision makers, this page comes in handy.

☐ ☐ ☐

NAMES OF ALL DECISION MAKERS:

BUDGET FOR PROPOSED SOLUTIONS:

Having your own fact-find packet or survey kit is essential for appearing to be different than the other insurance salespeople they have dealt with in the past. Just like a doctor, I'm going to take notes and listen closely. I will do this in front of my prospect so they know I really am listening and that I care!

So now, I will typically lead the conversation with a question like, "Mr. Jones, if you could change one thing about your current insurance program, what would it be?" If he refers to price and how rates go up every year, simply reply, "I understand, I feel the same way about my own insurance rates, but price aside, what would you change if you had a magic wand and price was not the concern?"

The prospect may respond with, "Nothing that I can think of." Well, that's a *safe phrase* because most prospects don't know what an excellent insurance experience looks and feels like. Dig in a little deeper by being more specific with your questioning.

Here are only three examples of how I would follow that response:

→ I see, have you ever had an issue with a payment or billing?

→ Have you ever called into your agency and left a message for your agent that never got returned?

→ Hmm, what coverages are most important to you?

TRANSITIONING INTO COVERAGE-SPECIFIC REVIEW AND PROBLEM IDENTIFICATION

I like to ask, "What coverages are most important to you?" because most prospects have no idea what their policy has coverage for and how it could have a direct impact on their business if a loss occurred. It's amazing to me how so many prospects I have met with tell me that they have never had their agent explain their policy to them in simple terms.

Your job is not to educate at this step; it is to <u>identify problems</u>. Focus on getting confirmation about what is important and determine if that need is being met in the policy. If it's not being met, it's time to find out just how important it is to the prospect that the problem be resolved.

They may initially respond, "Well, I just want to make sure I'm covered in case something goes wrong."

That's pretty vague. So I'll follow up with...

Me: "Have you ever had a claim?"

Prospect: "We did about 6-7 years ago."

Me: "What happened?"

Prospect: "Well, we had a partial fire in the kitchen, nothing too serious, but we were down for a bit."

Me: "Really? How long were you down?"

Prospect: "Hmm, I'd say about two weeks total."

Me: "Wow, how much money do you stand to lose when you're down for two weeks?"

Prospect: "During the time of year it happened? About $20,000."

Me: "How many meals do you have to prepare to put $20,000 into the bottom line?"

Prospect: "A lot that's for sure!"

Me: "Hmm... if we could find a way to make sure there is a pot of cash that we can reach into to recoup some of that lost income, and still keep your annual premiums in the budget, would that be important to you?"

Prospect: "Absolutely."

Me: "Ok, well let's put that on our list."

I work through each coverage by using "non-insurancese" so that my prospect can understand the problem he faces by not having a particular coverage. When you explain how a particular coverage can protect a prospect from what could be devastating, and really show the bottom line impact of not being prepared, it becomes an <u>emotional</u> issue.

If you just talk from a technical perspective on why it's important, they are never going to care or hear you. You must share stories and examples that are real and show how that problem could potentially put them out of business.

Keep in mind, I don't give the coverage name or solution away at all – I only <u>identify</u> the PROBLEM or PAIN – and I write each down on my list in front of the prospect. If you give away the solutions then all the prospect has to do is turn around and tell their agent, "Hey, could you price these coverages for me?" So now you did all the work for the incumbent, who isn't doing their job in the first place, and yet, they will probably keep the business because all things being equal – people don't want to switch. It's a hassle. Don't give away solutions, only identify problems.

Your objective is to gather no less than two, non-price related, solid problems or pains. They could be **service** issues, **relationship** issues, or **coverage** issues. If you can't identify at least two, non-price related issues then you must tell the prospect the following, "Mr. Jones, I don't see how I'm going to be able to help you improve your current insurance experience. It appears that your agent is doing a great job of servicing your needs, the coverage in your policy looks great, and to be honest, it's a fair premium. Am I missing anything?"

Mr. Jones may simply respond, "I guess not, I just wanted to see if you thought you could save me any money on my premiums." If that's the response, then I thank Mr. Jones for his time and let him know that if anything changes over the course of the next year or so he can feel free to call me. I'll also add him to my weekly ezine list (after getting his approval of course).

But let's assume Mr. Jones had several pains and problems. It's now time to recap what we've found. I will literally restate out loud the problems we identified together.

Me: "Mr. Jones, we've identified four problems that have either been a frustration or could put your business in a world of hurt if not resolved, and they are:

1. Your agent did not return your phone call.

2. You called in and the CSR acted like you were wasting her time.

3. You don't have the cash flow needed to make the large down payment at renewal, and have asked for other options but have never been given any solutions.

4. You currently have no coverage for paying ongoing expenses and key employees if down due to a covered claim."

He may help you clarify a certain problem or pain, but all you really want to do is make sure you have your list of diagnosed problems correct. At this point, he should be pretty upset and frustrated because of the problems you've helped him identify. Wouldn't you be frustrated? Depending on what all you've uncovered, he could be furious.

This is when you will start talking about their *insurance budget* because they are going to be more receptive to your "I'm probably not going to save you any money on your premiums" clause you stated at the beginning of your appointment.

#4 THE PROSPECT'S INSURANCE BUDGET

For some reason I used to hate talking about money with a prospect. I was hoping that after identifying a few major problems, I could just go fix them and present my solutions to them and they would hire me and fire the incumbent. But it didn't work out that way very often. What would happen is they would get my solutions and tell me they would like to "think about it."

When you can identify what the prospect thinks it should cost or would be willing to pay for the solutions on your list, then you can either come to an agreement about the budget in their mind and the budget you know it will probably take to solve the problems. I want to know we're on the same page before I do any work.

The most common response is, "Well, just come back with your best price and we'll see where we are at." If I have an idea of their budget, then I can gauge what level of coverage within each company I represent that I can offer them.

In some cases, you will have a business owner who will revert to the old school frame of mind of haggling over price with you. I don't engage in this either. I'm very straightforward, and it sounds like this, "Mr. Jones, the types of solutions we are looking for are going to put this kind of policy in the range of $20,000 to $30,000 per year in premium overall. Is that within your budget?"

Many of you are asking, "How do you know what price range to pick for this business, premiums vary from company to company!" Yes, they do vary, however they are typically in the same tier of premium overall. I use round numbers when talking about insurance premiums, if it's a small account, maybe you would use $5,000 to $10,000; or less if it's even smaller.

I need to know what they are currently paying; if they whitened out their premium figures on the declaration pages then I'm going to ask that they tell me in *round numbers*. *Round numbers* means to round up or down. Instead of $18,687.36 they would say $19,000.

Now, Mr. Jones has said, "Yes, that's in the budget," (let's assume for the moment) and you will move into confirming the 5th Key Point... are there any other decision makers?

#5 WHO MAKES THE FINAL DECISION?

Once Mr. Jones is in agreement about the budget, my next question is, "Mr. Jones, after I take this to my markets I'll be coming back with a proposal to share with you... is there anyone else who needs to be involved in the final decision?" The majority of the time there are not, but one time I made the mistake of never asking this only to learn that there were actually three partners, and they all showed up to the final presentation, much to my surprise.

Needless to say, the problems I solved satisfied the one partner I had my appointment with, but since I never took the time to ask if there was anyone else I should expect to meet with, I lost. Rather, I never had it in the first place and I learned to ask this before leaving future appointments.

This is a great time in your appointment to ask about the decision making process because we've established problems/pains and got a confirmation on moving forward within a budget. If there is anyone else to bring in, I need to know now and let's get them in here so my prospect can be in my corner while we're "in the moment."

Once we confirm that Mr. Jones is the only decision maker in this situation, what's next? I have heard this done several ways and I use a different version from time to time depending on who I'm talking to and what I feel will work best. The objective is to make sure everything is on the table...

THE "NO SURPRISES" CLAUSE...

Some of you want to know if this is a "close." No! Not in the traditional sense. Closes are out – they push people apart because prospects know what a close sounds like now. Remember, they have been conditioned over hundreds of years of cliché closes! The following phrase and inquiry is how I ensure that there are no more surprises out there that I need to know about before I leave this meeting. I have used both versions to bring out any final objections that may have been overlooked during the meeting. Simply use whichever you feel most comfortable using at the time.

Version #1
"So Mr. Jones, we've identified problems (1), (2), and (3); is there anything that would prevent us from doing business together if we can fix these problems and keep it in the budget we discussed?"

After I ask this, I don't say a word. I'm listening.

If Mr. Jones responds with, *"No, we should be good,"* I'm going to follow with, *"Let's assume we do end up moving forward together, somebody is going to have to give Bill* [the incumbent agent] *some bad news, are you comfortable doing that?"*

I ask this because I have been burnt a few times because some prospects will always give their current agent benefit of the doubt and a shot at trying to fix what you're fixing. This is why you can't give away solutions in the appointment. Only give away solutions after you are confident you have a sale.

I have found this to be one of the hardest questions to ask because I'm always afraid that the prospect will say, *"No, I don't think I can do that."* But to my surprise, more often than not they will reply, *"I'd be willing to do that, this is business."*

All I care about is determining if they have the stomach to do it because eventually they're going to run into the incumbent agent. It could be at a golf outing, at the next Rotary meeting, or one of any number of events locally. The last thing you want is to come in to the final presentation only to find out that the incumbent was able to convince Mr. Jones that he could make this up to him and undercut your efforts.

Version #2
This is a Sandler technique – and I really like it. I started using this and have found it to be a great way to help the prospect give me an indicator of where we are at this point.

"Mr. Jones, on a scale of 1 to 10, with 1 being you want me to get out of your office right now and 10 being you see us doing business together already, where are you at?"

If they respond "5" or less, you are in a lot of trouble.

But if they respond "6" or better then all you need to say in return is, *"What do I need to do to make that a '10'?"* And then listen and take notes.

And, once you do know what it is that would make their experience a "10", you just have to be able to assure them that you can deliver – the rest is dependent on your ability to follow through. I will always ask about their comfort level in telling the incumbent that they are going to be canceling their policy with them. It is just business, and most agents know not to act like a jerk to the client when they send over a cancellation request, but I want to know they are truly comfortable with that decision before I leave the appointment.

What I like most about this style of selling is that it's fair. It's not manipulative; if anything, it's the most forward and honest form of selling you can do. You are literally treating your prospect like a good doctor would a patient.

If you don't quarterback each opportunity with a prospect, then things will get messy and the whole time you're talking they will be thinking, "When is this guy going to try to close me," or, "I wonder how much this thing is going to cost me," or, "I bet he's just trying to up-sell me."

I always tell my prospects where we're headed. There must be an objective for the meeting so that no one is wasting their time, because time is your most valuable asset. If you can't find problems or pains at the beginning of your meeting, then politely tell the prospect that you won't be able to help them this year. I guarantee they will appreciate your professionalism and honesty.

The last thing I love about this style of selling is that there is hardly ever any reason to have doubt about the outcome of your final presentation. At the same time, I have had to meet with a prospect several times because we would only make it through the pains and problems stage at the first appointment. But at the end of that appointment, I would definitely tell my prospect where we were headed at the next appointment. "Mr. Jones, at our next meeting, I would like to discuss your insurance budget and all who are part of the final decision process."

Remember, there is no secret formula to selling, nor is there a script to memorize. It's about harmonizing, identifying problems, listening closely, caring, standing firm, and getting a commitment from the prospect for the hard work you are willing to do for them.

The way you have been selling up to this point probably has you "quoting" several prospects each month. I no longer subscribe to the Law of Averages. I'm not into throwing as many prospects against the wall to see who sticks. That is why prospects don't like dealing with insurance salespeople – because they have to say "no" since our price is not in line with what they wanted it to be. Your job is not to bring them a lower price. Your job is to solve problems.

By being completely honest with your prospect you will shock them and they will actually appreciate you more. Are you going to take as many prospects to market by using this sales philosophy? No. In fact, you may only end up taking 10% of the number of prospects you used to take to market. But your closing ratios will be more like 100% because at the end of the appointment you will have discussed everything you need to get confirmation for the sale.

13 | **Post-Appointment**

"Give us the tools and we will finish the job."

– Winston Churchill

THE RECAP LETTER

As soon as I get back to the office, I write out a recap of the problems we identified and create a *thank you* letter that addresses the problems we identified, the budget we discussed, and the next step (developing the proposal) and when we agreed to meet next.

I don't worry about the prospect sharing this letter with the incumbent agent for two reasons; (1) if he does share it with his agent, I haven't identified solutions yet, only the problems that we agreed were important... so the incumbent is going to feel pretty stupid; and (2) it's going to reaffirm in the incumbent's mind that I'm THE man. Worst case scenario, you just struck fear in that other agent's mind. Good for you.

TAKING THE PROSPECT TO MARKET

Agents complain all the time about how underwriting is hurting them... "They are so strict on guidelines!" or, "I can't get any quotes because they won't accept any risks I bring them." Stop complaining and blaming the companies you represent for your inability to properly identify what they are willing to competitively underwrite. Don't blame your market either. There are acceptable risks out there, you just have to find them. At this point in the book, however, you have found an ideal prospect that has agreed to your terms and is in need of solutions to several problems.

Your underwriters are part of your team and you should always be looking for ways to make their life easier. They deal with frustrated agents all day long on the phone from agents complaining and asking for "consideration" on gray-area accounts. I want to help you make a favorable and long-lasting positive impression on your underwriting team. **Secrets** below, straight from underwriters themselves!!!

UNDERWRITER SECRETS REVEALED!

On February 1st, 2011, I emailed several key underwriters I work with and asked for some insight. Here is what my email read:

> I am looking for some insight and advice from each of you regarding field underwriting and best practices that you have seen from producers or other agents. What are the top 10% doing that is making your life simpler? Could you reply with 3-5 suggestions for new producers that would help make YOUR LIFE SIMPLER as an underwriter or DM, as well as streamline the relationship and information process from field to company? Thank you.

Following these suggestions and those outlined on the previous pages in this step will earn you the respect of your underwriters, exceptions on certain accounts, and max credits in many cases. You've got to give first in order to get.

On the next few pages are a list of what you should be doing when field underwriting and submitting applications - clearly defined by underwriters. Remember, if you think it's value but your underwriter thinks it's crap... it's crap.

→ Familiarize yourself with company guidelines. We [underwriters] have a responsibility as a company to tell you what we write and don't write through underwriting guidelines, but it is up to the agent to review and learn them. This eliminates many declinations and the frustration of "they don't write anything". That is not true – you are just sending the wrong business to the wrong places.

→ Complete applications. Fill out all the blocks as best you can. There is a reason why all those questions are asked – the answers are important to the underwriting process.

→ Submit the correct application. Confusion only results when the wrong app is submitted. Sending in a CPP application when you want a BOP only causes confusion and frustration. Many times risks are eligible for both so we don't know you want a BOP if you submit as a CPP. We assume you know what you want and rarely will call or email asking if you really want this or that. We will not second guess you. Submit a cover letter for extra explanation if needed.

→ Visit the risk. If the risk has property coverage or has some size to it, you need to visit it and become familiar with it. Take photos while you are there and do cost estimators on most buildings (not so important on smaller risks). Talk with the prospect and tour it – become familiar with both the applicant and the business.

→ Respond in a timely manner to requests for additional information, inspection records, audits, etc. Nothing is more frustrating to an underwriter than an agent who appears to be ignoring him or her.

→ If you don't know the answer to a question, don't guess. If you don't know, that's fine. Find out the answer and get back with us. You gain more respect that way than "flying by the seat of your pants."

→ Strictly from a commercial standpoint, familiarize yourself with what information is needed for what kind of risk (such as contractors need payroll, mercantile businesses need sales, apartments need area and number of units, area for all others, and subcontractors need cost of hire). The various types of construction and their characteristics. This will take study on your own or attendance of Commercial Lines education/training.

→ The most important thing to me is a nice cover letter with an application explaining what the insured is doing/what the business is. All too often applications come in with either nothing in the remarks section or just "contractor". This leaves a lot of questions.

→ COPE: Construction, Occupancy, Protection Class, and Exposures

→ Loss history if possible – I know as agents this can be difficult to not tip off the incumbent, but very helpful and required in most instances.

→ Knowing what is in a company's "wheelhouse." For example, one company may want homeowners over age 65, with high insurance scores, clean auto support – average to above average business. This will help agents submit suitable business to the correct companies.

→ Timely follow-up with information to an underwriter is very much appreciated. For instance, if I ask for information on an insured and you have to call in to the insured and cannot get a hold of them for awhile, please let me know what you are doing so that I am not kept in the dark and keep asking for information.

→ Run all available reports (CLUE/MVRs etc.) if you intend on writing the business with a particular company. Nothing makes an underwriter, insured or agent more agitated than if we have to change tiers/cancel or increase premium due to a violation/claim that was not on an original application.

Remember the *Insurance Xperience Analysis Packet* in Step 6? Your underwriters may not know that is what you use when you go out on an appointment, but they would be proud and much more comfortable knowing you took that packet as opposed to the old yellow legal pad.

Here are some additional **secrets and techniques** I have used to provide my underwriters with the best underwriting information possible:

→ Take a Flip video tour of your account and email it to your underwriters.

→ At minimum, get several interior as well as exterior pictures for them.

→ Type up your ACORD forms.

→ Familiarize yourself with what is acceptable and quit calling in and asking for the moon on each account. Quit whining. Start sending qualified business their way.

→ Underwriters are on *your* side, but they are representing the company's best interests first. You, as the producer, probably think your first interest is the prospectful client, but it's not. Your FIRST interest is that of the company's.

→ Give them plenty of time to do their work. If you must have a speedy turn-around time on a proposal, call the underwriter(s) up and tell them about the situation, apologize and ask for their help. Don't simply email "Please RUSH" in the subject line with ACORDS attached. That's a quick recipe for frustrating underwriters. Unless of course, your underwriter has told you to do that in those cases.

THE PROPOSAL & FINAL PRESENTATION

Ed Lamont says that the proposal is simply a tool in the selling process. How many of you take your quote sheets out for a final presentation with a prospect? Oh, *what's that*? You have an Excel document your agency provides you with? You just enter in the data from the quote pages. That's lame too.

Lamont calls his proposal the ***Presentation of Solutions***. He prints it right on the front of the proposal. He also urges producers to include another recap letter on page 1 within the proposal and a snapshot overview on page 2 of *Problem*, *Solution*, and *Cost*.

So the first thing I do in my final presentation is begin by restating what we agreed to at our last meeting. I restate the problems we identified one at a time. I will talk about the budget one more time, "We also said that if we could fix these problems and keep it between $20,000 and $25,000 that we would be good to go. Does that sound right?" Get confirmation once again. Then tell them how much the thing costs! "Well, Mr. Jones, if we fix everything we talked about, I'm excited to say that we came in at $24, 374.21. The only thing that can happen now is that price will go down if you choose to not take one of the solutions we talked about being important." And then I go through the proposal, step-by-step. I ask questions. I listen. I'm not worried about losing the sale because I've gotten commitment from Mr. Jones throughout our entire courtship. We are both on the same page at this point and have been since day one.

"IT LOOKS REALLY GOOD..."

Sometimes though, you're not on the same page for whatever reason. Almost every single time – it's your fault. And if you don't address this objection in sheep's clothing, you will lose a sale. Here's how I would turn this objection into an opportunity to better understand what the real hesitation is at this point:

Prospect: "It looks really good, Matt. I'm just going to need a few days to think it over. I'll give you a call."

Me: "Sounds great, thanks for your time today. [as I begin packing up my stuff...] I've got a gut feeling I'm not showing you something you need to see. Are you concerned about the cost?"

Prospect: "No, that's not it at all."

Me: "What is the concern then, because you can tell me 'no' right now?"

Prospect: "Well, your agency isn't located in town here, it's not a deal breaker though."

Me: [After mentally kicking myself in the groin for not trying to determine this back in our initial appointment] "Do you mean not being *physically* present so you can stop in any time to pay your bill?" [You never know, it could be.]

Prospect: "No, I just like knowing that my agent is close by."

Me: "My cell phone is on my card and hopefully programmed in your phone. If I can assure you that your call would be answered within the fourth ring, anytime, would that put your mind at ease?"

Prospect: "Well, I'm not saying I'd be calling after hours, but yeah, it would be important."

Me: "Consider it done. Can we move forward now?"

If you get an 'I want to think it over' at the end of your presentation, you have to face the fact that you haven't shown this person the value in doing business with you yet. And now it's probably too late. If you had done a good job of identifying problems and pains that the prospect agreed needed to be fixed; discussed the budget and got confirmation that they are the decision maker; and you were able to deliver – there is really no reason for them to 'want to think it over.' Think back to the last prospect you worked with – did they tell you they wanted to think it over and get back to you? I guarantee you didn't cover the three areas above with them, and if you did… well then, it's all about value. And in their mind, you weren't bringing the best overall value to the table – and that hurts. Learn from it.

If you go into your final presentation and get the final total premium out of the way first, I would be sure to state at that time, "Mr. Jones, I appreciate the opportunity to work with you on developing these solutions, but I would also appreciate that at the end of this presentation you tell me, "Yes, we're in business Matt," or, "No Matt, this is not what I wanted to see and I'm going to stay where I'm at." I don't mind you telling me "No," I just don't want to hear that you need time to think about it. Is that fair?" I think that's fair and if you've identified the key points outlined in this Pillar then you should have no problem in getting a clear "Yes" or "No." Hopefully, you are getting an enthusiastic "Yes!"

✗CHALLENGE | PRACTICE MAKES PERFECT

When would you like to know that the prospect is not going to buy from you despite the problems you solve, because price is the only thing that matters? Before you invest 30-40 minutes talking with them and another day of working up ACORD forms and discussing the risk with underwriters, and putting it into a proposal form, and preparing your notes for your presentation, etc? Exactly. I want to know right now, up front.

The purpose of this exercise is to get you used to identifying ideal prospects and their problems/pains, selling on value, and not price. You must train yourself to think in terms of helping prospects solve problems – if you can't solve any problems (aside from price), then walk away from the opportunity to quote. It's an empowering feeling, and a professional act.

Step 1 | Make a list of 50 very low-premium commercial accounts (target premium range of $1,000-$5,000 annually).

Step 2 | Follow the sales philosophy and outline above for engaging each prospect. Begin with your sales letter and mailing. Follow up with a phone call. Get used to hearing objections and responding with questions that help refine the objection. Don't think of these as sales calls, these are interviews. You are interviewing the prospect to determine if you are going to be a good fit for helping them solve problems. Your objective is to obtain an appointment.

Step 3 | Out of the 50 who made the initial list, your goal is to obtain 10 appointments. In these appointments be sure to build positive rapport immediately and then lay it out on the desk for the prospect, "Mr. Jones, I just want to outline the objective I have here today and make sure you feel that it's fair. First, I'm probably not going to be able to save you any money on your insurance premiums, what I hope to do is determine if there are any problems that you have in your current insurance experience. If we find some problems then we can move forward in the appointment if we haven't run out of time or you feel we can do so at this time. If we can't find any problems other than price, then I can leave and we can keep in touch if anything changes down the road. Does that sound fair to you?"

Are you going to state it word for word like that? No, of course not. But you must make those key points and obtain an agreement for moving forward at this point. If the prospect says, "No, that's not fair," (which I have had happen before), then just dismiss yourself politely. Stand your ground. Get used to saying "no" to quoting opportunities.

Out of the 10 appointments you booked, you should probably only go to market for about 1-2 prospects. But you should be leaving your appointment knowing the terms outlined in this Pillar as important and be confident that you have the sale.

PILLAR V

"SERVICE"

IS FOR UNDERSTANDING
SERVICE, CLIENT LOYALTY AND
THE LIFE CYCLE OF A CLIENT

14 | **Screw Customer Satisfaction**

"Satisfied customers will shop anywhere..."

– Jeffrey Gitomer,
www.gitomer.com

If I read one more insurance billboard or advertisement claiming to have the highest rating in customer satisfaction, I'm going to puke all over my dashboard.

I swear – what does it mean to have a satisfied customer? It means you do exactly what the customer has grown to expect from you. That could be a lot of things for a lot of different people; and in my opinion, *satisfied customers* do a whole lot of shopping around when prices go up.

Insureds have come to expect meager levels of service and automated systems. The bar for excellence is not set that high to begin with in regards to delivering excellent service in this industry.

I have asked numerous insureds what **excellent customer service** means to them and here is what I discovered:

→ Return my phone call promptly.

→ Tell me when rates increase and why – did I do something wrong?

→ Answer the phone like you enjoy what you do.

→ Give me solutions, not excuses.

→ Don't have to lower premiums each year, just be proactive and shop my policies on occasion. Then, let me know what you discovered, even if it means you don't have anything better. I just like knowing you are looking out for my bottom line.

→ Explain what my policy protects me from – use simple words.

- → Give me options if possible.

- → Touch base at least once per year to see if there is anything that needs to be changed – my life is busy and insurance is the last thing I think about.

- → Christmas cards are a nice touch.

This list is not all-inclusive, but do you notice anything on this list that is out of the realm of possibility based on our job description? This is not excellent customer service in my opinion – it's simply service. **Excellent customer service** appears to be nothing more than providing solutions to insurance problems, at a fair premium, and responding to any and all problems/concerns in the most efficient manner possible. That's it.

Please note that in order to provide solutions to problems we must both (me and the client) be in agreement about the problem we are trying solve. If they don't perceive it to be a problem, then I'm not doing my job. That <u>is</u> service!

But you don't return phone calls. You don't shop them and show them what you've found out. You wait until they call you, angry and ready to leave.

Now, I understand that your top 20% get attention and care. That's always going to be that way. However, we need to establish some basic practices that we can commit to in order to ensure that each insured feels needed and appreciated.

CREATING THE *ULTIMATE* INSURANCE XPERIENCE

To create an experience for an insured, one that causes them to be positively changed, as well as stop and think about you, takes a willingness to do more than is expected. As we can see and attest to, great customer service would only require us to do our job right.

Creating The Insurance *X*perience does NOT mean you must lower premiums each year – that's impossible and a fallacy.

What can you do to differentiate yourself from the guy down the street selling the same policies? This is beyond developing a personal brand. I'm talking about one-sided generosity in action; creativity on purpose; and strategic initiatives that cause the insured to stop and think in terms of you.

Do you have to spend a lot of money to be creative and gift an experience to an insured? Not at all. It's like when you used to make a construction paper card for your mom and she would cry when she saw it and read it. It's the thought. Start thinking.

I love the story of Johnny the Bagger (**stservicemovie.com**), a 19-year old grocery store bagger with Down Syndrome, who proved that creating customer loyalty is simple when you truly care.

Johnny asked his father to help him type up inspirational and thought-provoking quotes, and cut them out into tiny squares so he could drop one in each customer's bag as they went through his line.

The result? The grocery store manager noticed one day that Johnny's line had all of the customers lined up... and there were other lines still open! They tried to get the customers to move to the open lines to improve efficiency (an attempt to keep customers *satisfied*) but they would not. They told the manager they were waiting for a piece of Johnny's wisdom. Wow.

The store manager noted that business actually began to improve as a result. Not only did Johnny secure his position for life (and I hope a bonus), but he selflessly created an experience for the customer that cost him nothing more than the time to type up a quote and cut it out. The act of the gift is when he dropped it in their bag – it became a nice surprise for the customer. It changed the climate of the day. That's the power of a gift.

Close your eyes and envision what kind of experience you could create for insureds if there were no limitations. Would you roll out red carpet in your cubicle? Would you jump up from your desk and trot over to greet them with an enthusiastic handshake and smile? Would you walk them to the door?

Here are few other ideas for creating an experience...

→ Instead of your lame office Christmas card, create a video with your Flip camera and email it to your clients. Be fun.

→ Text each client on their birthday, saying, "Heyyyyyyyoooooo! Canon Ball! Happy birthday!" (or improvise...)

→ Cut out anything about their business or family that makes print media (i.e. newspaper or magazine) and mail it to them with a card congratulating them. The only exception would be if they made the Police Reports section... or not.

→ Know each client (and member of their family) by first name and call them by name each time you see them.

→ Create a monthly ezine or online newsletter that is unique and of value.

→ Call up each client and simply thank them for their business, no hidden agenda.

→ Use wrapping paper to wrap new policies and mail to insureds, like a gift!

→ Promote all commercial clients on your Facebook page.

→ Interview all commercial clients for a tip about their business that would be helpful for their ideal customer and share via your YouTube Channel.

→ Print off a thought-provoking quote that inspires or sparks positivity and include in each outgoing envelope to clients.

→ Create a referral incentive program that is focused on recognizing clients who refer qualified business to you!

Creating loyal customers is all about relationship. If you aren't taking the time to develop a relationship with your insureds then they will be satisfied customers... who shop around.

I remember reading Ken Blanchard's *Raving Fans: A Revolutionary Approach to Customer Service* in undergrad and took away one thing – the difference is in the details. Keywords include authentic, genuine, proactive, helpful and passionate. Raving Fans are customers who are so moved by what you do that they feel compelled to share their experience with their network and sphere of influence (AKA "friends").

This becomes more than a referral because raving fans sell you to the other person. They are mini-ambassadors on your behalf. They become apostles spreading the good word about you. They become part of your sales force.

15 | The Insured Life Cycle

"Do what you do so well that they will want
to see it again and bring their friends."

– Walt Disney

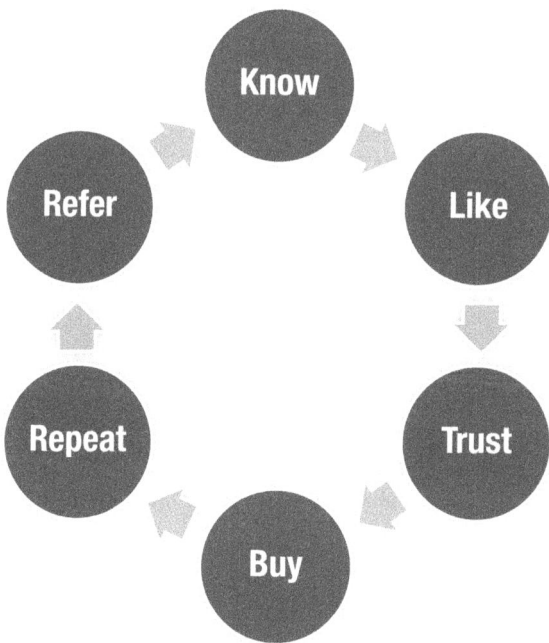

The Insured Lifecycle (tailored from that of John Jantsch's Ideal Customer Life-cycle from his book The Referral Engine, www.referralenginebook.com) is simply a way of understanding the typical process that insureds travel through in their journey with you. They buy in their time frame. Keep that in mind.

You can't speed along a sale without causing them to feel rushed into a decision. At the same time, however, you can use positive energy to keep business moving.

Here's a brief overview of each step in the cycle:

1. **Know** – advertising, media, social media, networking, word of mouth, community
2. **Like** – dig deeper, online investigator, ask others
3. **Trust** – sign up for your ezine, third party introductions, agrees to meet
4. **Buy** – expectations are everything, *the buying experience*, the tools (proposal) you use
5. **Repeat** – cross-sell, help them get the most out of your product/service (how-to materials)
6. **Refer** – end result, ambassadors for your business, apostles of your product/service

Know

The statement, 'It's not what you know, it's who you know,' is garbage. It doesn't matter who YOU know at all. The only thing that matters is WHO knows you, and more importantly, what do they know about you!

Your advertising, media and marketing materials are the basis of this stage. This is your first impression point, and like all first impressions, it's important to make it a good one.

To make it easier on both you and your potential customer, it is also imperative that you clearly define the type of customer you are looking to reach.

The more specific you are about *who you are* and *who you help*, the easier it is going to be to qualify new leads (prospects). Everything about your communications should be geared towards this ideal customer.

Like

This stage is critical. Why is it important that someone 'like' me (and my business) in order to buy from me? Isn't it more important that they 'trust' me? Isn't it more likely that they will buy from me if they trust me?

No. The simple fact is that we base every purchase decision emotionally at first, then logically. A single girl goes out on a date with a guy and says (or thinks to herself), "I really like this guy," and begins to determine how much she thinks she can trust him.

She's not going to say, "I really trust this guy... I wonder how much I like him?" Doesn't happen that way. You are either likeable, or you're not. And if you're not likeable, then you should get out of insurance sales.

After you have popped up on someone's radar, they will most likely begin to dig a little deeper before initiating contact. This leads most of us to our computer and the web. Google. Facebook. Linkedin. We'll poke around your website, your Facebook Page, and your profile.

This stage has a dual responsibility; your online presence should be reflective (once again) of the type of customer you do business with. And this helps pre-qualify (at a deeper level) the prospective customer.

While poking around online they will begin to identify with you and what you do, or they won't. This is great for you because the more clear you are about whom you can help, the more receptive this prospective buyer becomes at the next stage.

Trust

Trust is established in several ways. Sometimes it's after meeting in person several times at the same events or locations; such as committee meetings, golf course, networking event, bar, etc. But there are also different levels of trust. Many times we *borrow* trust. A mutual connection talks about us behind our back to a potential new client and they begin to trust us without having actually met us yet.

Once someone begins to like you and has had time to digest 'you' online in an unobtrusive manner, assuming you are Googleable, they may take the next step and sign-up for your ezine.

My offline strategies, coupled with my online presence has led to a greater deal of trust with prospects before I even meet with them to discuss insurance. Those that opt-in for my weekly value ezine are potentially ideal clients for me. I've identified what "value" means for the clients I get along with best and love sharing ideas that help them produce and profit more.

The cool part about clearly identifying value for your ideal prospect and then delivering it consistently (through an ezine, for example) is that you begin to activate the law of attraction. I've received dozens of replies to my ezines from individuals asking about homeowners insurance, professional liability insurance, auto insurance, commercial insurance referrals, and so on. They're reaching out because they began to **know** more about me, and as a result they **liked** me, which led to them **trusting** me enough to opt-in for my ezine. An inbox is a busy place and if you're not investing your time to create compelling and unique message that helps your subscriber produce more immediately, they are going to click over you. The trust you earn from a prospect is not something to take lightly – it's a privilege. Trusting leads to more sales, which leads to your income!"

Buy

The buying process is critical for solidifying your new relationship. The proposal you bring with you to the final presentation and how you present are tools that cause the buyer to think, say and sign "yes" on the dotted line. Your letters, video, inspection of the account, the questions you ask; all of these are tools for creating value in the buyer's mind. They must feel like you are the best at what you do – because you are!

Repeat

Studies have shown that cross-selling a client leads to longer retention rates. It's a fact. But don't go in with a hidden agenda, thinking that if you can get them to buy an umbrella policy all of sudden you've got a loyal client. Doesn't work that way. Your intention should always be to help the insured solve problems.

Insurance solutions evolve over the course of a person's (or business') life. Our job is to be <u>proactive</u> with those solutions. This means we remain in contact throughout the year and identify areas where we should increase or decrease coverages. But stop thinking that cross-selling is about retention; instead, it's about **helping**.

Refer

This is the best part of the cycle. Referrals are what almost every business is about – and this is especially true in insurance. We live for the referral! By implementing the strategies, formulas, techniques and principles in this book, you should have no problem maintaining a steady pipeline full of teed-up referrals.

Your clients become apostles of YOU, spreading the good word and stories of your amazing works throughout your market. Keep your energy flowing through your market and you will reap amazing benefits through referrals.

There are leads organizations at most chambers of commerce; or an organization like BNI (**www.bni.com**) has proven to be very beneficial for millions of professionals. I have also heard of many people simply starting their own leads group – just do your research.

Summary

The insured life cycle is not set in stone. Nothing ever is. You can learn how to engage insureds and maximize prospects' buying motives by listening to your current clients. Focus on your clients and give them a reason to talk about you to all their friends. If you're likeable you've got half the battle won already – but if they don't trust you, they won't buy from you.

When a friend tells a prospect you're awesome and they would be a fool for not doing business with you – that's power. Now you don't have to sell, because people will want to buy.

16 | How to Offer a 100% Guarantee That Sells

"In business you get what you want by giving other people what they want."

– Alice MacDougall

This concept of guarantee-selling is nothing new, but it is to our industry. In fact, almost any industry could benefit from this one simple strategy for eliminating doubt from your buyer's mind. I guarantee, in fact, that if you implement this into your overall strategy you will undoubtedly increase your sales. I can make that kind of guarantee because I have already implemented it into my own strategy, only to experience the same positive effect.

Here's what I recommend you do:

Call up the last five prospects who did NOT buy from you. Be genuinely interested when you ask, "Mr. Jones, I know you chose to not do business with me and I'm completely fine with that decision, but I want to get better at what I do. I want to help more people with their insurance problems but in order to do that I need to know what it is that causes someone to either buy, or not buy, from me. Or from any insurance agent for that matter! What do you look for in *your* insurance agent? What's <u>most</u> <u>important</u> to you, all B.S. aside? What three to five things do you consider seal the deal for an insurance agent striving to win your business?"

Of course, this is not a script, but you get the idea. The objective is to assure the prospect or client that you lost, that you are not calling them up to try and get their business back. You are reaching out to them for perspective. You genuinely want to improve and need their help. You want to know what would cause them to feel most comfortable and akin to buying from an insurance agent, price aside. If they bring up price and nothing else matters to them, then you have called the wrong ex-prospect for advice.

This is difficult to do because most people will be honest with you when they sense you are genuinely interested in improving yourself and your service. It's difficult because it hurts to hear how you could have delivered the "value" that particular prospect wanted to see.

The good news is that once you ask about five ex-prospects or clients these questions and start gathering bullet points of "value" then you will notice a consistency and common theme.

Here is an example of what you could have uncovered in interviewing commercial prospects and ex-clients:

1. I want to know my insurance agent is experienced and knowledgeable in managing the risks associated with my particular business.

2. I want to know my insurance agent is a leader among his colleagues and is passionate about what he does.

3. I want my insurance agent to return my phone calls or emails promptly.

4. I want to know that my insurance agent is going to be there when I need him, after the sale.

5. I want to know that my agent is an independent agent who can offer me a reasonably priced policy year after year with a company that has strong financial strength.

6. I want to know that the company my insurance agent has placed my business with is going to be able to pay covered claims promptly.

7. I want to know that I have options for my bill pay plan. I can't afford a large down payment at this time of year because of cash flow.

These are, essentially, seven guarantees that you could make that most commercial prospects would find to be of value. You must create a business card or mini-pamphlet with these guarantees, calling it *7 Things You Should Know Before You Hire Your Next Insurance Agent*. Put your contact information or a bio on the pamphlet as well and use it as your new business card.

How much more powerful would your business card be if it were a *guarantee card*? The challenge is to deliver on whatever guarantees you discover are important to the prospects you are trying to reach. Different ideal prospects have different definitions of value.

By this point in our journey through this book, you should have clearly defined who your ideal prospect is and where you can find them. The only thing left to do is to ask them what would help them eliminate their concern or delay in buying from an insurance agent. Find the consistencies among the prospects you are reaching out to.

CONCLUSION

This book was written to be used as a self-help resource, not shelf-help. Don't simply put this on your book shelf and feel good about the ideas that have been shared in here. The only way you're going to rise to the top 10% of your market, change your insured's experience, and take your success to the next level, is by taking immediate action and implementing the ideas you've learned.

It is my ultimate desire that we, as young insurance professionals, can infuse our industry with positive energy and ideas that will not only alter the way business is done, but the perceptions of our business at the same time. Instead of "quoting" and leveraging the Law of Averages, become a risk doctor and diagnose patients. Find their pains and heal them if you are able to. If you are not able to heal them of their pains, be a professional and tell them you can't heal them! In fact, recommend them to a specialist – this could be another agent you have developed a good relationship with that specializes in a particular area of insurance that you know would be able to better help your patient... whoops... prospect.

I will make you two guarantees:

(1) When you stop quoting and start interviewing for pains and problems with a prospect, you will lose the opportunity to work on as many proposals as you have in the past...

(2) But... when you stop quoting and start interviewing for pains and problems with a prospect, they will notice that you are different. They will begin to recognize you as a person of value because you are the most honest agent they have ever dealt with. They will appreciate your passion, integrity and authenticity.

Will you take less prospects to market in the end? Yes. But will your closing ratio be more towards 100%? Yes.

I would rather work on two accounts this week using a smart and professional method of selling where I knew I was able to help the insured <u>and</u> earn a commission, than on seven or eight accounts where I had no idea if I was going to be able to help because I didn't properly identify *value*. I'm confident you feel the same way!

To your success!
Matt Brown

P.S. If you found this book to be of value please email me at *matt@mattmbrown.com*. I do check and respond to all emails.

P.P.S. I'd also love to connect with you on Linkedin, Google+, and all other social networks.

✖CHALLENGE | RANDOM ONE-SIDED GENEROSITY

You need to get into the habit of practicing generosity without expectation for a return. At the end of one week you will feel more joy and inner peace by doing the following acts – make it a part of your daily life to simply give.

Do the following on each day of the next week.

Monday | Go buy a coffee (or whatever you drink in the morning) and tell the cashier you are giving them $5 to buy the next person's coffee or beverage. Tell the cashier they can put the rest in the tip bowl or change tray.

Tuesday | Compliment EACH person you have an interaction with. This is harder than it seems. Make a brief comment on how great they look; hair, tie, shirt, pants (take it easy), and so forth. Or maybe they did something really great last week and you could tell them how awesome they did. Perhaps you can thank someone for helping you when they did, even if it was several weeks ago – just let them know you truly appreciated it. Each person you have an interaction with.

Wednesday | Volunteer to read to elementary students at a local school in your community for 30 minutes.

Thursday | Listen to one person vent about something that is frustrating them in their life. Listen intently. People will talk for 20 minutes if you let them. Let this person vent it all out. Then hug it up with them. (The only exception to this rule is if the person is venting about how their marriage is on the rocks and they are of the opposite sex of you – this could be misconstrued and actually get you into a lot of trouble). But a genuine hug and offering of your ear and attention is gold.

Friday | Buy donuts for your agency – not just the glazed ones either – those suck. Get the filled sticks and sprinkles and everything. Get options.

Get a lot of options. Get a box of coffee as well. Take them in early to the office and just set them out in the common area (wherever that is in your agency).

Then go to your cubicle or office and act like nothing happened. If they ask where they came from just say you felt like partying on a Friday morning. Don't stand around for the compliments and thank yous.

Acknowledgements

Thank you to my heavenly Father who has provided me with countless gifts and blessings, and Who has also helped me take on a new mind over the past several years – but let's be honest, we both know I still have a long way to go. Thank you for Your patience.

My smokin' hot wife and best friend, Megan. I don't deserve someone as fun, kind, inspiring and awesome as you, and I am honored to share this life with you.

To my sons Jackson, Aidin and Collin – you make life rich and fun. You are the joys of my life. I love you guys.

Thank you to Dwight and Jane Brown, my parents who have always encouraged me to walk to my own beat. To my sister Laura, you have a huge heart and I envy you for that. To Janis, my mother-in-law, for all of your love and continued support.

To all extended family, I appreciate you always being supportive of me regardless of my unassuming nature. Thank you.

To my Aunt Phyllis, Grandma Brown, brother-in-law Nathan Carse, and countless other friends and family members who have joined the heavenly ranks. I'm not afraid of dying anymore, I'm only afraid of not *truly* living – and each of you have shown me how. I am eternally grateful for your examples.

Thank you to my clients for appreciating my value and creativity. In an industry where the lowest premium wins, you give hope to our new economy where true success is measured by how much one gives, rather than how much one slashes prices.

To anyone who has invested this book – the simple act of investing in my book or to hear me speak or train, reaffirms my major definite purpose in life... and for that, I thank you.

Bibliography

Chopra, Deepak. *The Book of Secrets: Unlocking the Hidden Dimensions of Your Life.* Three Rivers Press, 2005

Chopra, Deepak. *The Seven Spiritual Laws of Success: A Practical Guide to the Fulfillment of Your Dreams.* New World Library/Amber-Allen Publishing, 1994

Dyer, Wayne W. (with M.D. Deepak Chopra). *How to Get What You Really, Really, Really, Really Want.* Audio Book: Hay House, 1998

Ferriss, Timothy. *The 4-Hour Work Week.* Crown Archetype, 2009

Gitomer, Jeffrey. *Little Black Book of Connections.* Bard Press, 2006

Gitomer, Jeffrey. *Little Gold Book of YES! Attitude.* FT Press, 2006

Gitomer, Jeffrey. *Little Red Book of Sales Answers.* FT Press, 2006

Gitomer, Jeffrey. *The Sales Bible.* Wiley, 2003

Godin, Seth. *Linchpin: Are You Indispensable.* Portfolio Hardcover, 2010

Groves, Eric. *The Constant Contact Guide to Email Marketing.* Wiley, 2009

Hill, Napoleon. *Think & Grow Rich.* Tribeca books, 2011

Holy Bible: New International Version. Grand Rapids, MI: Zondervan, 1978

Hyde, Lewis. *The Gift: Creativity and the Artist in the Modern World.* Vintage, 2007

Jantsch, John. *The Referral Engine: Teaching Your Business To Market Itself.* Portfolio Hardcover, 2010

Lamont, Edwin L. *Street Smart Selling: Beliefs, Strategies, and Management Ideas of Successful Insurance Professionals.* The National Alliance Research Academy, 2009

Michalko, Michael. *Thinkertoys.* Ten Speed Press, 2006

Peale, Norman Vincent. *The Power of Positive Thinking.* Fireside, 2003

Solis, Brian. *Engage!* Wiley, 2011.

Tracy, Brian. *Goals! How to Get Everything You Want – Faster Than You Ever Thought Possible.* Berret-Koehler Publishers, 2006

Tracy, Brian. *Speak to Win.* AMACOM, 2008

The National Alliance for Insurance Education & Research. *Dynamics of Selling Audio Series.* The National Alliance Research Academy, 2008.

ABOUT THE AUTHOR

Matt Brown was nominated for the prestigious *Rough Notes* Magazine and *National Association of Professional Insurance Agents Young Insurance Professional of the Year Award* after only one year in the insurance industry. He has been featured as a Next-Gen leader in *PIA Ohio Magazine* and has been interviewed by Peter van Aartrijk and Rick Morgan on *InsuranceJournal.TV*'s *On Point Podcast Series* to discuss his marketing and sales strategies.

Matt is a Producer with Hill & Hamilton Insurance and Financial Services located in Ohio. He is also a highly sought-after private coach to Main Street producers across the country, as well as a speaker on the topics of Marketing, Sales, and Peak Performance. He also serves as a marketing and sales strategist to several companies located in Ohio.

He is married to his college flame Megan, they have three sons and reside in Ada, Ohio.

He is 28 years old.

Connect with and learn more about the author at his website,

www.MattMBrown.com

Index

Costanza, George; 91
Council; 111
country; 25, 32
county; XXIV
cover; 26, 114, 116, 141, 165, 180, 182, 193, 197, 222
coverage(s); XVII, 5, 77, 80, 81, 117, 131, 148, 157, 162, 166, 171, 175, 179, 181-183, 193, 217
CPP (Commercial Package Policy); 193
credibility; 115, 125, 150
credit(s); 83, 131, 142, 192
creed; 37
crisis; 20
critic(s)(al); 8, 67, 128, 171, 215-216
CSR (Customer Service Rep); 59, 66, 70, 82, 153, 182
culture; 135
customer; XI, XVII, 134-135, 205-209, 213-215

D
danger(ous); XXIII, 141
data; 6, 34, 53, 67, 83, 142, 168, 171-172, 176, 195
database; 34, 120, 150
deadline; 33, 39, 52-54, 58-59, 65, 68-69, 82, 90
death; XXIV, 6, 105
debate; 126, 166
Decca Recording Company; 90
decision; XXIII, XXIV, 11, 31, 109, 153, 171, 183-184, 186, 213, 215, 221
decision maker; 34-35, 67, 148-149, 159, 160, 166, 167, 171, 173, 178, 183-184, 197
declaration; 183
department; 162
dependent; 186
dialogue; 9, 13, 127, 131
DIY; 81, 116-117, 131
DNA; 95
doctor; 93, 155, 160, 165, 169, 172, 179, 186, 223
document; 195
dollar(s); 13, 84, 112, 117, 119, 125, 130, 134, 151
domain; 113
donations; 105

dream(s); XVII, XVIII, 29, 33, 134
Dyer, Wayne; XXII

E
earn; XVIII, XXIII-XXIV, 9, 29, 31-34, 37, 39, 57, 78, 82, 84, 92, 100, 118, 123, 128, 136, 192, 216, 224
economical; 49, 133
economist; 51
economy; XXII, 79, 81, 105, 123, 230
education; XXIII, 130, 193
eHow.com; 112
elementary; 225, 229
elixir; 38
email; 7, 9-10, 12, 49, 64-65, 67-70, 72, 82, 91, 93-94, 96, 101-103, 111, 113, 116-120, 125, 127-128, 133, 152, 192-195, 208, 222, 224
emergency; 69-70
Emerson, Ralph Waldo; 51
Entertainment; 130
entrepreneur(s); 52, 102, 128
environment; XXIII, 19
excellence; 134, 205
executive(s); 52, 63-64, 94, 130, 152-153
expense(s); 10, 112, 118, 131, 141, 182
expert(ise); 30, 77-79, 90, 94, 104-105, 123-124

ezine; 70, 81, 99, 116-118, 120, 125, 133-134, 152, 181, 208, 214, 216

F
Facebook; 10, 34, 49-50, 69, 82, 112-113, 115, 123, 125-127, 133-134, 136, 149-150, 208, 215
factory; 79
failure; 6-7, 38, 112, 125
fair; 39, 80, 162, 166, 169, 181, 186, 197-199, 206
faith; XXII, 25-26, 36-40
fallacy; 206
family; XXII, XXIII, 18, 116, 123, 141, 161, 172, 208, 229
FAQs; 81
fear, afraid; 7, 41, 96, 106, 185, 229
fitness; 35
Ford, Henry; 90
forefathers; 143-144
Forgiveness; 20

Franciscan University; 230
fraud; 5
friendship; 20, 160, 161, 166

G
Gahanna (OH); XXI
gatekeeper; 160
genius; 97, 101
Ginsberg, Scott; 92
Gitomer, Jeffrey; XXI-XXII, 15, 23, 91, 98, 125, 143, 203
global; 126
gmail; 68, 113
God; 30, 38, 52, 107
Godin, Seth; XXII, 6, 83, 113, 147
Google; XXI, 5, 25, 34, 68, 111, 131-132, 134, 149, 215-216, 224
gratitude; 78

H
Hammurabi; 141
handshake; 21, 166, 207
Hanley, Ryan M.; XIV, 78
Hays Insurance; 90, 153, 235
Hill, Napoleon; XXII, 18, 30, 38
Holtz, Lou; 108
homeowner, homeowners insurance; XVII, 81-82, 97, 117, 147, 152, 194, 216
Hondros College; 230
honesty; 129, 186
hospital(s); 165
Hubbard, Elbert; 112
Hyde, Lewis; 79

I
image(s); 77, 91, 144
imbalance; 51
incorporate; 26, 130
incumbent; 42, 53, 181-182, 185-186, 191, 193
index; 40
indicator; 185
individual(s); XXIV, 5, 52, 79, 103-104, 109, 111, 117, 147-148, 152, 176, 216
industrial; 79, 123
industry; XI-XII, XIV, XVIII, XXI-XXIV, 6, 9, 14, 22, 29-30, 32, 38, 41, 79, 80, 84, 89, 102, 106, 113-114, 123, 126, 141-142, 147-148, 165, 205, 221, 223, 230, 235

inflation; 64
influence; 18-19, 107, 209
information; 97, 103, 114, 120, 127, 149, 152, 160, 172, 192-194, 223
Insurance Quadrant of Art; 21, 77
international; 5
internet; 123, 149
intrinsic; 77, 80
invest; XVII, XXII, 18, 33, 78, 92, 113, 118-119, 158, 166, 198, 216, 230
investment; XXII, 92, 97, 113, 125, 134
islands; 80
Israel; 37
Italian; 51
Italy; 51

J
Jantsch, John; 213
jargon; 153

K
Kelly, Zander; 95
Kennedy, James J.; XVII
Kenton Middle School; 229
Kenton High School; 229
Kiwanis; 151
Kula; 80, 82

L
Lamont, Ed; XIII, XXII, 84, 143, 158, 195
law; 52, 104, 141
Law of Attraction; XXII, 103, 120, 125, 216
Law of Averages; 142, 165, 187, 223
lawyer; 55
leader; XI-XII, XIX, XXIII, 12, 50, 71, 96, 101, 103, 112, 115, 222, 235
leadership; XXIII, 100, 105
leads; 119-120, 147, 150-151, 214, 217
liability; 84, 98, 155, 157, 160, 216
liberation of content; 126
library; 18, 81
Limbic System; 6-11
Linchpin; 6, 83
Linkedin; 34, 70, 93, 94, 102-103, 113, 115, 125, 127, 149-150, 215, 224
Lions; 51, 105, 111, 151
"lizard brain"; 6-9, 40
loan(s); XXIII, 104

Louisiana State University; XXIII
loyal(ty); 8, 125, 135, 207-208, 216
Luke; 36

M

magazine; 113-115, 151, 153, 156, 208, 235
Malinchak, James; XI, 69
management; XII-XIII, XVIII, 6, 61, 63, 81, 158
mandate; 89
manifest; 25, 101, 102
Mark; 36
market(s)(ing); XIII, XVIII-XIX, XXII, XXV, 6, 7, 14, 19, 29-30, 32, 34-35, 50, 52, 67, 70-71, 82, 84, 89, 95-96, 100-102, 104-105, 111-112, 115-116, 119, 120, 123, 127, 129-130, 135, 149, 152, 165, 170, 183, 187, 191, 199, 214, 217, 223-224
marketplace; 30, 85, 89, 94
Marketsource Agency Network; 230
marriage; XXI, 225
Mashable; 132
McPheron, Alisa; 102
media; XXII, 50, 69-70, 78, 82, 111, 116, 120-121, 123-128, 132, 133, 135, 151-152, 156, 159, 167, 208, 214, 235
Medieval; 141
meeting(s); 7, 50, 53, 65-67, 100-101, 103, 150, 161-162, 166-170, 184-186, 195, 215
Mehrabian, Albert; 107
mercantile; 193
Michalko, Michael; 41
Michigan; 14
Microsoft Word; 66, 172
Millennial generation; 49
Miller, Dennis; 95
money; XI, XXII, 13, 18, 30, 32, 40, 57, 69, 79, 100, 106, 123, 125, 129, 142, 149, 150, 156, 158, 168-170, 180-182, 198, 207
MVR (Motor Vehicle Report); 194

N

national; 22, 133, 235
network(s)(ing); XIII, 18, 78, 92, 94, 96-97, 99, 101, 104, 113, 116, 123, 127, 133, 150-151, 167, 209, 214-215, 224
the news; 22, 127
Nightingale, Earl; XXII, XXIV

Northwood Elementary School; 229
notoriety; 101, 114

O

objective(s); XXIV, 7, 66, 92, 125, 149, 162, 167, 181, 184, 186, 198, 221
Occam's Razor; 47
organization; 49, 81, 82

P

Pareto Principle; 51
Parkinson's Law; 52-54, 70
St. Paul; 11, 133
Peale, Norman Vincent; XXII, 18
Penny, James Cash; 27
PIA (National Association of Professional Insurance Agents); XXI, XXIII, 22, 114, 115, 230, 235
Pixar; 22
polic(y)(ies); 5-6, 13-14, 31, 34, 49, 51, 69, 77-81, 83-84, 117-118, 124, 128, 136, 142-143, 147-148, 155, 157, 162, 165, 171, 175, 179-181, 183, 186, 205, 207-208, 216, 222
power question; 98-99
practice; XXI, 12-13, 108-109, 111, 198
prayer; XXV, 20, 36, 38
prehistoric thinking; 3-14
premium; XXIV, 9, 13, 31-32, 34, 39, 51-52, 78-79, 84, 117-118, 142, 153, 168-170, 180-183, 194, 197-198, 205-206, 230
priority; 116
privilege; 124, 126, 216
producer; XXIV, XXV, 13, 26, 29, 31-32, 49, 66, 82, 93, 102, 104, 116-117, 120, 126, 147, 153, 158, 168, 192, 194, 195
product(s); XVII, XXII, 26, 35, 79, 80, 84, 101-102, 142, 144, 148, 151, 158, 214
productiv(e)(ity); XXII, 21, 50, 53, 63, 64, 70, 99, 105, 126, 127, 130
profession; 95, 142, 169-170
professional(s)(ism); 10, 21, 30, 36, 52, 53, 66-67, 70, 77-79, 81, 89, 94, 95, 97, 99, 100, 112-115, 128, 130, 135, 142, 152, 154, 158, 165-166, 170-171, 175, 186, 198, 216-217, 223-224, 235
profit(able); 52, 78-79, 81, 94, 99, 105, 116, 118, 125, 129-130, 136, 156, 216
program(s); 151, 155, 169, 179, 208

project(s); 7, 8, 53, 66, 68, 71, 105, 116
property; XVII, XXI, 53, 98, 155, 160, 193
prospect(s); XXII, XXIV, 7-8, 11-14, 17-18, 26, 32, 34, 39, 42, 43, 50, 52-54, 57, 65, 71, 79, 85, 89, 96, 98-100, 114, 117, 125, 127, 130, 133, 142-144, 147-157, 159-162, 165-169, 171-174, 176, 179-187, 191, 193-199, 214, 216-217, 221-224

protect(ion); XVII, 84, 93, 97-99, 117, 143, 149, 155, 159, 166, 175, 181, 193, 205
psychology; 167

Q
qualified business, qualified prospects; 96, 99, 194, 208
qualify(ing); 99, 149, 214
quality; 30, 53, 57, 119, 120, 142, 150
quantity; 119
quota; XXIV, 30-32, 50
quote; 6, 9, 10, 50, 66, 79-80, 89-90, 96, 100, 106, 130, 132, 142, 153, 155, 158, 168, 170-171, 191, 195, 198, 207-208

R
Rankin, Johnathan; 102
rapport; 115, 125, 160, 167, 171, 198
rate(s); XXII, 32-33, 64, 179, 205, 216
ratio(s); 116, 171, 187, 224
reader(s); XII, 78, 112, 116, 153
realtor(s); 14
recommendation; 23, 150, 171
record; 89-90, 129, 131, 193
recoup; 180
recruit; 105
refer(ral)(ence); XI, XVIII, 5-6, 20, 22, 34, 129, 136, 151, 159, 167, 169, 179, 208-209, 213-214, 216-217, 234
reject(ion); 7, 17, 41, 43, 90, 106
relationship(s); XI, XVIII, 52, 84, 94, 115, 135, 158, 162, 166, 168, 181, 192, 208, 216, 223
reputation; 10, 71, 105
revenue(s); 32, 54
Richards, Charles; XVII, XXIV, 6, 8, 35, 55
risk(s)(y); 81-82, 92-93, 141, 169, 176, 191, 193, 198, 222-223
ROI (Return on Investment); 134

Romans; 11
Rotary; 51, 78, 105, 111, 151, 185

S
sale(s); XVII, XXI-XXII, XXIV, 7, 10-11, 13-14, 17-19, 23, 29-30, 34, 39-40, 42-43, 51, 70, 77-79, 82, 96, 98-99, 102, 105, 112, 116, 118, 124, 127-128, 130, 135, 142-144, 148, 153-157, 159-160, 162, 165-167, 176, 185, 187, 193, 195-196, 198-199, 209, 213, 215-216, 221-222
salespeople, salesperson(s); 8-9, 125, 142-144, 153, 158, 169, 170, 179, 187
Sandler, David; XXII, 143, 145, 168, 185
satisf(y)(action); 35, 184, 205-209
save; XXI, 35, 50, 64, 70, 82, 100, 115, 127, 129, 133, 142, 158, 168-170, 181-182, 198
savings; 170
science; 38
secur(e)(ity); 8, 123, 207
social security number; 142, 176
Seinfeld, Jerry; 21, 91, 105
seminar; XII, XXI, XXV, 34, 91, 168
service; 29, 39-40, 52, 66-67, 83, 102, 116-117, 120, 123, 154, 174, 181, 205-214
Seuss, Dr.; 153
share(s); XII, XXIII-XXV, 14, 38, 57, 64, 69, 77-78, 80, 83-84, 90, 92, 99, 103-104, 106, 108, 110-112, 114, 116, 120, 125-127, 129-131, 134, 156, 158, 166-167, 181, 183, 191, 208-209, 223, 229
Shaw, George Bernard; 3
skill; XIII, 7, 49, 107, 111, 113
speaker; XI-XII, 69, 96, 106, 107, 110-111
specialist; 117, 148, 223
speech; 14, 106, 108-109
spiritual; 38
Steubenville (OH); 230
strateg(y)(ies)(ic); XIII, XXV, 11-12, 18-19, 29, 53, 57, 69, 71, 78, 82, 90, 92, 108, 112, 116, 125-126, 130, 133, 135-136, 147, 150-152, 158, 207, 216-217, 221
subjective; 41
success(ful); XXI-XXII, XXIV-XXV, 6, 10, 14, 23, 25-26, 29, 33, 36, 38-40, 50-51, 53, 83, 95, 102, 104, 108, 111, 123, 127-128, 133, 156, 158, 223, 230

survival; 6
system; 6-7, 11, 25, 49-50, 66, 127, 132, 144, 165, 167, 205

T
taboo; 143
tax; 176
team(mates); 53, 128, 134, 191-192, 230
technique(s); XXII, XXV, 21, 23, 29, 43, 59, 96, 99, 107, 109, 151, 158, 185, 194, 217
television, TV; 21-22
testimonial(s); 128-129
Thinkertoys; 41
Thomas, Fred; 78
Tracy, Brian; XXII, 33, 70, 108-109, 111
trade; 141, 151
tradesman; 141-142
transaction; 78, 80, 83-84, 126
transfer; 40
transforms; 38
transition; 20, 40, 123, 179
transparency; 132
Trump, Donald; 19
Twitter; 94, 115, 127, 132, 134, 149
typepad; 113

U
UCLA; 107
undercut; 185
underwrit(e)(er)(ing); XXII, 6, 19, 35, 49, 53, 68, 148-150, 172, 191-195, 198, 230
university; XXIII, 102, 111, 229-230

V
vacation; 63, 70, 72
Vaughn, Vince; 13
visualize; 26
voicemail; 8, 89-91, 96
volunteer; XXIII, 7, 42, 104-105, 151, 225

W
Walker, Trent; 13
Wall Street Journal; 78-79, 130
Wapakoneta (OH); 116
Wodicka, Jeff; XXII, 143
wordpress; 113

Y
Yahoo!; 68, 113
YIP (Young Insurance Professional); XIX, XXIII, XXV, 6, 10, 21, 36, 38, 53, 66-67, 70, 77-78, 81, 89, 95, 100, 112, 115, 135, 142, 165, 171, 223, 235
YouTube; 78, 81, 91, 93-94, 130, 149, 208

Z
Ziglar, Zig; XXII, 14, 18, 23, 90, 143

www.ingramcontent.com/pod-product-compliance
Lightning Source LLC
LaVergne TN
LVHW051459080426
835509LV00017B/1820